Mysterious Lands and Peoples

Mysterious Lands and Peoples

By the Editors of Time-Life Books

TIME-LIFE BOOKS, ALEXANDRIA, VIRGINIA

CONTENTS

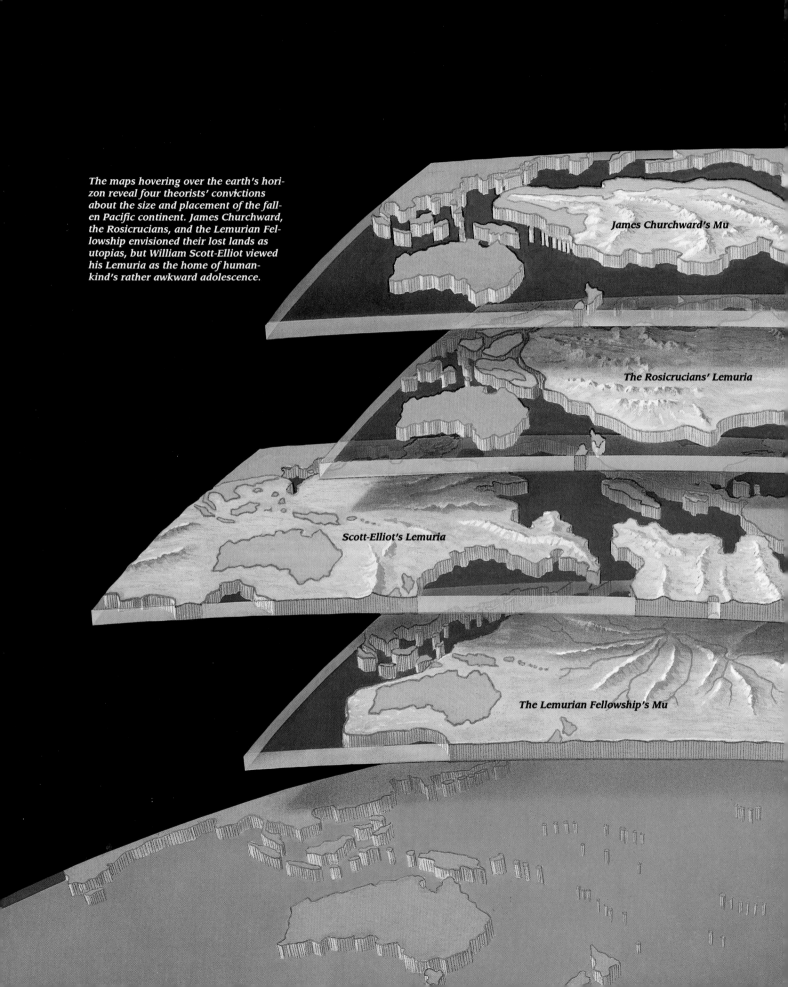

The maps hovering over the earth's horizon reveal four theorists' convictions about the size and placement of the fallen Pacific continent. James Churchward, the Rosicrucians, and the Lemurian Fellowship envisioned their lost lands as utopias, but William Scott-Elliot viewed his Lemuria as the home of humankind's rather awkward adolescence.

James Churchward's Mu

The Rosicrucians' Lemuria

Scott-Elliot's Lemuria

The Lemurian Fellowship's Mu

Dreams of a Lost Pacific Home

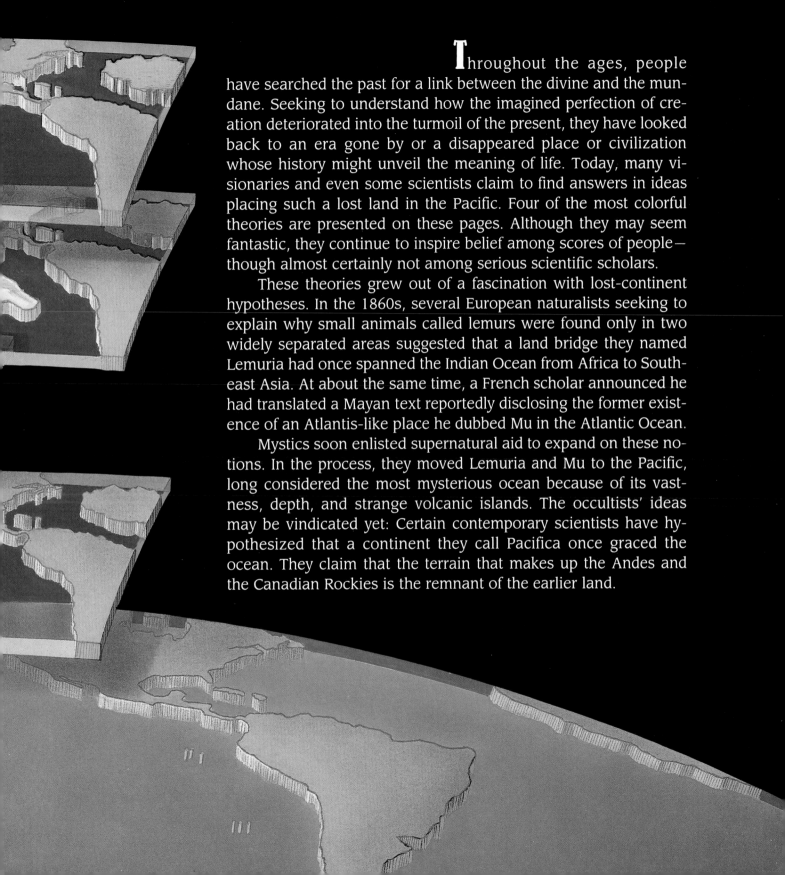

Throughout the ages, people have searched the past for a link between the divine and the mundane. Seeking to understand how the imagined perfection of creation deteriorated into the turmoil of the present, they have looked back to an era gone by or a disappeared place or civilization whose history might unveil the meaning of life. Today, many visionaries and even some scientists claim to find answers in ideas placing such a lost land in the Pacific. Four of the most colorful theories are presented on these pages. Although they may seem fantastic, they continue to inspire belief among scores of people—though almost certainly not among serious scientific scholars.

These theories grew out of a fascination with lost-continent hypotheses. In the 1860s, several European naturalists seeking to explain why small animals called lemurs were found only in two widely separated areas suggested that a land bridge they named Lemuria had once spanned the Indian Ocean from Africa to Southeast Asia. At about the same time, a French scholar announced he had translated a Mayan text reportedly disclosing the former existence of an Atlantis-like place he dubbed Mu in the Atlantic Ocean.

Mystics soon enlisted supernatural aid to expand on these notions. In the process, they moved Lemuria and Mu to the Pacific, long considered the most mysterious ocean because of its vastness, depth, and strange volcanic islands. The occultists' ideas may be vindicated yet: Certain contemporary scientists have hypothesized that a continent they call Pacifica once graced the ocean. They claim that the terrain that makes up the Andes and the Canadian Rockies is the remnant of the earlier land.

A Short-Lived Tropical Paradise

''The Garden of Eden was not in Asia but on a now sunken continent in the Pacific Ocean.'' So begins Anglo-American James Churchward's *The Lost Continent of Mu,* a 1926 book that tells the fantastic history of one man's paradise lost.

Churchward claimed he learned of Mu while supervising famine relief in India during the late nineteenth century. There he forged a fast friendship with a Hindu priest who, Churchward said, led him to some hidden tablets inscribed in an ancient tongue called Naacal. The two men supposedly pored over the enigmatic writings side by side, ultimately employing psychic powers to understand their remarkable contents.

According to Churchward, the tablets—which have since mysteriously disappeared—said that Mu stretched 3,000 miles in length and 5,000 in width. Replete with rolling, well-irrigated plains and lush vegetation, its geography provided an aesthetically pleasing backdrop for a highly developed and wealthy people. The Muvians plied the seven seas to trade and colonize and reached unparalleled heights in the fields of science, technology, and education.

Mu's upper classes enjoyed a refined lifestyle of leisure and comfort, adorning themselves with opulent raiments and dazzling gemstones. The dominant Muvian race, the author repeatedly stated, was white, reigning supreme over peoples of other skin colors.

Churchward's British Empire gone tropical was short lived, however, finally destroyed by volcanic eruptions, earthquakes, and tidal waves. A few shards of the sunken continent remained above water, forming the Pacific islands, and some of the Muvians clung to these, reduced to cannibalism in order to survive.

Psychic Gifts of the Lemurians

In diametric opposition to James Church-ward's capitalistic Mu, the land that American Rosicrucian Wishar Cervé described in his 1931 book, *Lemuria: The Lost Continent of the Pacific,* housed an utterly nonmaterialistic people whose foremost goal was spiritual development.

The book's preface tells that Cervé learned the true history of the Lemurians from some ancient Tibetan and Chinese manuscripts that conveniently appeared in the Rosicrucian Brotherhood's San Francisco offices. These tracts divulged that the Lemurians possessed a physical feature unknown to humans today. A walnut-size protuberance from their high foreheads—Cervé linked it to the modern-day pituitary gland—enabled them to communicate telepathically, to perceive objects and beings in their "fourth dimension," and to see the past, present, and future. It also allowed them to converse with animals, as seen here in a telepathic exchange between three Lemurians and a saber-toothed tiger.

Cervé wrote that volcanic eruptions and earthquakes gradually submerged the western part of Lemuria, driving many of its inhabitants east. This eastern region eventually split from the mainland to form Java, Sumatra, Australia, and New Zealand, as well as part of California.

Pureblood Lemurians are still thought to dwell on California's Mount Shasta, having built a village inside that dormant volcano. People peering through telescopes have allegedly discerned lights glimmering atop the mountain and, ever so rarely, a majestic-looking Lemurian or a herd of primordial cattle on the slopes. However, all attempts to study the Shasta community have failed because the Lemurians, says Cervé, use their sixth sense to shroud themselves in invisibility.

An Evolutionary False Start

Although the flamboyant mystic and Theosophical Society founder Helena Petrovna Blavatsky discussed the lost Pacific continent of Lemuria in her 1888 tome, *The Secret Doctrine,* it was her ardent follower William Scott-Elliot who gave complete form to her ideas. In a 1904 tract called *The Lost Lemuria,* he tried to marry the Darwinian theories of the day with the cosmic wisdom of Theosophy's omniscient Tibetan mahatmas.

Scott-Elliot described a Lemuria that "nearly girdled the globe." Most of its feeble-minded inhabitants were twelve to fifteen feet tall. Inordinately wide-set eyes gave them superior peripheral vision, and a third eye at the back of the head—the pineal gland in today's humans may be its vestige—completed their 360-degree view of the world. It also guided them when they walked backward on extended heels evolved expressly for that purpose. They killed animals for food, training small dinosaurs as hunting companions.

The first Lemurians, Scott-Elliot wrote, were hermaphrodites and could reproduce without a partner. Over time, however, they developed sexual reproduction, though not without a few false starts: During the nascent stages of their heterosexuality, they confusedly mated with animals, producing today's great apes. This bestiality so offended the Lhas—the gods who had created the Lemurians—that they abdicated their thrones.

Lemuria would not remain untended for long, though, for Venusian wizards with schemes for converting their dimwitted charges into intelligent immortals soon replaced the Lhas. The metamorphosis was precluded, oddly enough, by the same phenomenon that destroyed Churchward's Mu and Cervé's Lemuria: volcanic eruptions that sank the continent.

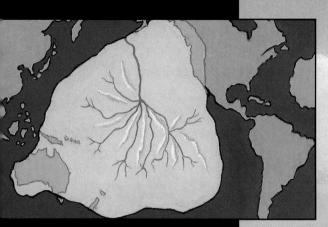

Democracy Forged and Forfeited

Distinguishing its own claims from "the fancifully grotesque tales" that others wrote about the lost Pacific continent, the Lemurian Fellowship published a series of books in the 1950s that purportedly chronicle the real history of Mu.

The first of these books, *The Sun Rises,* charts the birth of a nation. In the beginning, it relates, Mu was an anarchic collection of uncooperative factions. The Plains Dwellers, Forest Dwellers, and Cave Dwellers varied remarkably in height and talent. All had skills, but mutual fear and mistrust prevented them from cooperating. To improve the situation, the sagacious Elders of Mu chose two young Plains Dwellers, Rhu and Hut, to lead a reform movement.

The youths rallied members of all groups around a common goal, the building of a bridge to reach an expanse of rich farmland. Out of this unity, a political utopia—the Mukulian Empire—grew on the fertile terrain beyond the bridge. Its ten laws—which read curiously like principles of modern liberal politics—included that "no man shall profit at the expense of another" and that "every citizen shall be entitled to receive equal education, equal opportunity, and equal standing."

The empire gained such renown that people flocked to it from all over the continent. At first, rigorous citizenship training was required of newcomers, but rapid economic growth soon made the procedure unwieldy. Noncitizens were then admitted as laborers, which wrought such havoc that the idyllic order was destroyed, and the continent, as if in response to the empire's political strife, vanished into the depths. But the story did not end there: According to the Lemurian Fellowship, Mu would rise from its watery grave on May 5 in the year 2000.

CHAPTER 1

A Past Full of Shadows

ometime in the first century BC, a heavy-laden Grecian vessel was crossing the straits that cleave the isle of Crete from the rocky peninsula of the Peloponnese, when it was caught up in a terrible storm and began to break apart. In the turmoil of the moment, the crew of the foundering craft may have escaped to the nearby islet of Antikythera with a few valuables, but the bulk of the ship's cargo, consisting mostly of bronze and marble statuary, vanished beneath the waves of the Aegean Sea. There, these noble wares remained for nearly 2,000 years.

In 1900, sponge fishermen diving off the shores of Antikythera happened upon the silt-covered bones of the ship. Among the prizes that they hauled up from the wreck were four corroded chunks of bronze, apparently the fragments of a single object. Along with other artifacts, the bronze lumps were consigned to the National Archaeological Museum in Athens for further study. Close examination revealed that they were actually clusters of gears. The object was obviously a machine, probably a navigational instrument of some kind.

Fifty years later, a Yale University history professor named Derek de Solla Price became intrigued by the fractured artifact and was granted permission to explore its innards by employing x-rays and gamma rays. The device turned out to be far more intricate than anyone had imagined. The professor discovered that it was made up of no fewer than thirty-nine gears enmeshed on parallel planes and set in motion by a toothed turntable. As de Solla Price scrutinized the ratios of the gears and their mode of interaction, he was led to an unavoidable but astonishing conclusion: The device seemed to be a kind of analog computer that had been built to predict the movements of the Sun, the Moon, and the planets Mercury, Venus, Mars, Jupiter, and Saturn.

In its original form, the instrument was probably housed in a wooden box that measured twelve by six by three inches. The gears were turned by cranking a handle once a day. Three dials served to display the predictions: One of them showed the position of the sun in the zodiac (its path through the heavens) for every day of the year; a second dial chronicled an eighteen-year cycle of solar eclipses; and a third dial traced the various phases of the moon.

De Solla Price provided a detailed description of the remarkable mechanism in an article published in a 1974 issue of *Transactions,* the journal of the American Philosophical Society, and he advanced a date for its manufacture of about 87 BC. Calling the device "an elegant demonstration or simulation of the heavens," he asserted that "this singular artifact, the only complicated mechanical device we have from antiquity, quite changes our ideas about the Greeks and makes visible a more continuous historical evolution of one of the most important main lines that lead to our modern civilization."

In other words, the ancient Greeks were not quite who they were thought to be. Previously they were seen as brilliant theoreticians about the workings of nature but disinclined to pursue practical applications of their insights. However, the celestial computer—one of "the greatest basic mechanical inventions of all time," in de Solla Price's view—emphatically demonstrated that their heads did not always remain in the clouds. It was a marvel of applied science. The device not only required an intimate knowledge of the heavens, it also showed a level of technical acumen that was centuries ahead of its supposed time. One feature was truly stunning: The central turntable of the mechanism functioned as a differential gear train—an arrangement that allows shafts to rotate at different speeds. Until the corroded trophy from the Aegean revealed its secrets, such a gear design had been considered an invention of the seventeenth century.

In a sense, scholars were simply running true to form in underestimating the Greeks. Over the past century or so, the study of history has brought a series of radical corrections and reappraisals. While most researchers have contented themselves with incrementally sharpening the focus of their picture of humankind's forward progress, some scholars have, in effect, changed the lens, greatly widening the view to reveal links, precedents, and broad patterns that were previously invisible. Over and over again, historical and archaeological orthodoxy has been shaken by revelations of human precocity. Columbus, it turns out, was beaten to the New World by Norse seafarers, who established a small settlement in Newfoundland in AD 986. Similarly, the spherical nature of the earth was not first discovered during the Renaissance, as generations of students were taught; 2,000 or more years earlier, the Greeks and Indians independently arrived at the same conclusion.

Other jolting surprises came to light from the realm of prehistory: Archaeologists found that, more than 5,000 years ago, supposedly benighted tribes in western Europe were building immense stone complexes that functioned as calendars, marking key celestial events such as the winter solstice with great accuracy. But human genius had begun to express itself thousands of years before the era of Europe's timekeeping megaliths. For instance, a series of astonishing finds in limestone caves in France and Spain revealed that the Cro-Magnon forebears of modern humans created dazzlingly lifelike paintings of animals as early as 17,000 years ago.

Even as the record of cultural achievement underwent a series of major adjust-

A first-century-BC version of an analog computer, the so-called Antikythera mechanism—shown below with a replica (left) that was reconstructed by archaeologists—mimicked the movements of the heavens. The device may have been inspired by a planetarium created 200 years earlier by the Greek mathematician and inventor Archimedes.

ments, the tenure of the human species itself was extended far back in time. Most nineteenth-century scientists measured the human past in terms of thousands of years. However, recent finds indicate that at least 1.5 million years ago an ancestral line that came to be known as *Homo erectus* took up stones, bones, and sticks and shaped them into tools to be used for assorted purposes. Evidence unearthed in East Africa reveals that bands of early humans carried out organized butchery of wild game at least one million years ago.

Revolutionary discoveries are often less than welcome. Resistance or outright denial are common reactions—understandably enough, since whole careers can be reduced to irrelevance by a new finding. But in many cases, the solidity of the evidence has been decisive. Buried implements, old hearths, fossils, dating methods that use the atomic decay of carbon or rock to tell time—these and other sorts of proof have been virtually irresistible in many of the challenges to mainstream views.

Well-grounded proof is not always available, of course. On some issues, historians and archaeologists stand in an uncomfortable middle ground, caught between a sense that their current understanding of the past is not quite correct (or perhaps even utterly wrong) and a countervailing sense that caution is proper. In this middle ground, true-or-false judgments may lie forever out of reach. Speculation will have to suffice.

Temptations to speculate boldly are everywhere. For example, some iconoclastic thinkers believe that there is truth to the legend of King Arthur or of King Solomon's mines or of the vanished land of Atlantis—just as there turned out to be a real Troy, scene of the Greek poet Homer's timeless epic, the *Iliad*. Some researchers are fascinated by scraps of evidence hinting that Roman seafarers reached North America in ancient times or that Egyptians landed in Australia or that voyagers from various Asian cultures visited the civilizations of South America thousands of years ago. Most historians dismiss such ideas as fanciful—or certainly far from proven. But practically all would agree that, more than ever before, the study of the past is rich in mysteries.

The very nature of human progress is one compelling puzzle. Is it evolutionary, a gradual accretion of knowledge? Or does it sometimes occur in explosive rushes, great leaps of achievement that are followed by utter collapse—and the subsequent obliteration of virtually all signs of genius by the scouring passage of time? Proponents of this less orderly scheme of development maintain that a few surviving texts, rock paintings, structures, and other clues attest to the existence of brilliant and powerful civilizations in the distant past—hundreds of thousands of years ago, or perhaps millions. These theorists also venture the notion that some cultural supernovas may have blazed with blinding glory in the comparatively recent past, only to fade unaccountably into darkness again. The Maya of Mesoamerica are one likely candidate.

Around 500 BC, the Maya made their appearance in the rain forest of Guatemala. Theirs was an exotic land, a dim, green region of tall ceiba and mahogany trees, hung with vines and loud with the calls of monkeys and vividly colored birds. In this forest dominion, the Maya began digging drainage canals and clearing fields for corn and other crops.

It was not long before whole cities began to rise; some would eventually have a population of 100,000 or more. At their centers, great stepped pyramids towered above the jungle canopy. Shrines at the pyramids' pinnacles were roofed with arches, the only example of this architectural feature in the Americas. The surfaces of the pyramids and surrounding temples were elaborately carved with images of gods and nobles, and the sculpted figures were stuccoed over and painted in bright hues. Most of these figures were depicted in spectacular garb—cloaks tailored out of parrot and macaw feathers and the skins of jaguars, enormous headdresses, and a profusion of ornaments fashioned from shell and jade. In the background swarmed imagery of all the richness of the jungle—its flowers, turtles, snails, birds, and vines.

Even as they advanced the arts of farming, architecture, and ornamentation, the Maya devised the only complete writing system in the Americas—a combination of phonetic symbols and pictographs that has never been fully deciphered. They also developed surpassing proficiency in the fields of mathematics and astronomy. The zero, a crucial tool for advanced calculations, was one of their inventions. Their numerical system, which was far more flexible than that of the Romans, was based on twenty digits, denoted in dots and bars. With this computational system, they were able to devise a calendar like none ever seen on earth. It consisted of seven interlocking cycles of time, including a solar year of 365 days, a ceremonial year of 260 days, a lunar cycle, a cycle for Venus, and two other cycles whose significance has never been determined. Running concurrently at different rates, these cycles interacted to form a calendar that repeated every fifty-two years, spinning out toward eternity. But beneath the repetition lay infinite variety: Every single day, from the beginning of time to the end, had its own unique numerical characteristics.

This much is known. But what is not known? Is it possible that deeper layers of wisdom and numerical genius are hidden in those partially deciphered writings or in some geometric characteristic of their temples? And why, after exploding onto the stage of history and fashioning a culture of such magnificence and potency, did the Maya abruptly abandon their cities several hundred years before the arrival of the Europeans? For the moment, the haunted cities of the Maya guard their secrets well.

Mysteries also abound at Mohenjo-Daro, or the "mound of the dead," a vast urban complex that sits atop an arid bluff flanking the Indus River, which winds through Pakistan. In this sprawling city of kiln-dried brick, a highly evolved society flourished nearly 5,000 years ago. Along with a sister stronghold to the north named Harappa, Mohenjo-Daro probably dominated the entire Indus River basin, an enormous territory that extended from the Himalayan foothills to the Arabian Sea. Factory-size grain-threshing floors and storage facilities indicate that Mohenjo-Daro had a centralized state economy that afforded a high standard of living to its citizens—about 40,000 of them at its peak.

The metropolis was a masterpiece of rigorous design. Paved streets ran through row upon row of brick town houses, all of them fitted with indoor plumbing and served by an elaborate and unique sanitation system that consisted of chutes, clay pipes, and brick-lined drains. The rulers of Mohenjo-Daro, drawing on skillful metallurgists, developed state-of-the-art arsenals of spears, axes, daggers, and maces, while well-to-do residents boasted jewelry of gold, silver, and copper inlaid with ivory and precious stones. The raw materials needed for these creations were imported all the way from the Himalayas, Persia, and the distant reaches of India. Traders from the city benefited from a lucrative export business as well, selling ivory, jewelry, and cotton cloth—which, in all the world, the Indus people alone knew how to make.

In spite of its many accomplishments and its seeming cohesion, the Indus civilization toppled sometime around 1700 BC, felled perhaps by Aryan invaders who swept down onto the Indian subcontinent from the Eurasian plateau. Piles of skeletons found in postures of extreme distress at several spots around Mohenjo-Daro may have been the handiwork of the exultant Aryan conquerors, whose exploits are chronicled in the pages of the classic Hindu text the Rig-Veda. However, only scant written information has been retrieved from the sepulchral city, in the form of inscrutable inscriptions on fragments of pottery and soapstone, and scholars cannot say with certainty why the Indus civilization collapsed.

Its fate has been the subject of some startling speculations. In the 1930s, a Belgian linguist named Guillaume de Hevesy declared that the script of the Indus Valley

Equipped with functional wheels, this clay animal is one of several such figurines found in Mexican tombs dating from the first century AD. Discovered in the 1940s, the animals shattered the longstanding assumption that New World inhabitants had no knowledge of the wheel prior to the era of Spanish colonialism.

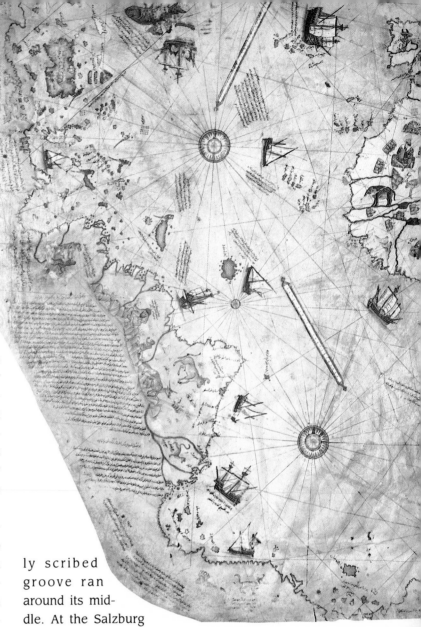

culture bears a marked resemblance to the undeciphered writings of another now-vanished people—the inhabitants of Easter Island, who, for reasons unknown, lined the shores of their mid-Pacific world with enormous statues *(page 85).* Did some survivors of the fallen Indus Valley culture make their way across Asia and thousands of miles of ocean to begin again in a new home? Few scholars accept such a connection. Fewer still find merit in another speculation about the fate of Mohenjo-Daro—the notion, inspired by the technological achievements of its people, that the Indus Valley civilization was destroyed by a nuclear holocaust. Among other difficulties, the time factor works against the nuclear scenario. Mohenjo-Daro lies only a few millennia back in time—not far enough for the years to have erased the signs of such an event.

Yet the time factor can work in favor of some unorthodox ideas about the past. When looked at with respect to the sweep of the planet's 4.5-billion-year lifespan, the sum total of evidence contained in the archaeological record appears minuscule indeed. Like a few fluttering candles in an immense desert at night, hard facts illuminate only tiny areas in the expanse. So limited a body of evidence opens the possibility that the interpretations founded on that evidence can be off the mark—or maybe fundamentally wrong. This possibility is a critical link in the logic of those who believe that the technological attainments of recent millennia merely recapitulate forgotten periods of genius in the darkness of eons gone by.

But the holders of such views do not build their case only on the poorly surveyed vastness of time or on ambiguous hints in ancient manuscripts and the like. There is, they say, some tangible and incontrovertible evidence—a number of peculiar objects that seem to have slipped through a time warp.

In 1885, for example, a clump of coal broken open at an Austrian foundry not far from the industrial city of Salzburg was found to contain a metal object about the size of a baseball and weighing just under two pounds. It was roughly cubic, but two of its sides bulged slightly. An evenly scribed groove ran around its middle. At the Salzburg Museum, where the object was taken for examination, physicist Karl Gurls had no doubts that this chunk of steel and nickel alloy was machine made. But whose machinery could have created it? The coal within which the block allegedly had been sealed was dated to the Tertiary period, which meant that the object could be 66.4 million years at the oldest, and 1.6 million years at the youngest. The Salzburg Cube, as it was dubbed, promptly went on display but disappeared from the museum's collection in 1910 and has not resurfaced.

An equally perplexing item was reportedly found in 1961 in a mountainous region of California. Three amateur rock collectors were on a scouting trip in the rugged Coso foothills along the east flank of the Sierra Nevada when they happened upon a rounded specimen that appeared likely to be a half-million-year-old geode—a hollow rock lined with brilliant mineral crystals. According to their account, one of the three, Mike Mikesell, sliced the specimen

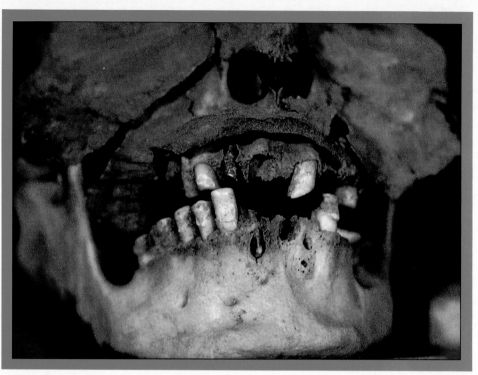

open the next day with a diamond saw. Inside he found an agatelike quartz that had been packed around a three-quarter-inch-wide cylinder made of what appeared to be fine-grained porcelain. Protruding from the cylinder was a metal rod that was, oddly enough, magnetized. Hoping to learn more, Mikesell sent the specimen to the International Fortean Organization, located in Arlington, Virginia, which is dedicated to the study of anomalous artifacts. X-rays revealed that a metal spring was attached to the still-embedded end of the cylinder, along with fragments of copper rings that had once encircled the ceramic rod. In short, the item contained within the 500,000-year-old stone bore an uncanny resemblance to the modern-day spark plug.

The Coso find would seem to imply that, in the dim reaches of time, a race of beings on the North American continent had somehow reached a level of technology matching or surpassing that of the twentieth century. Doubters point out, however, that normal geologic processes can act with enough speed to explain the crystal-encased spark plug.

Even in the conventional scheme of human progress, the technology for crafting intricate items from metal was mastered far back in the past. Seven thousand years ago, Mesopotamian peoples had developed this skill. Metal-working facilities also apparently existed at other Eurasian sites very early on. Soviet archaeologists in 1968 stumbled upon an ancient foundry near what is now the Armenian village of Medzamor, within sight of the mystical Buyuk Agri Dagh, or Mount Ararat, long held to be the landing place of the biblical patriarch Noah and his creature-laden ark. Here, 4,500 years ago, workers wearing protective masks and gloves stoked some 200 furnaces and smelted ore to produce copper, lead, zinc, iron, gold, tin, manganese, and fourteen different bronze alloys. Their output included everything from metallic paints to weapons to jew-

elry. In the trove was one eerily modern item—a pair of steel tweezers.

From a grave in China comes an even more curious anachronism, a belt fastener taken from the burial robes of the Jin dynasty general Chiou Chu, who died in AD 316. Analysis of the curious openwork fastener has shown that the artifact is composed primarily of aluminum, with some copper and manganese mixed in. The refining of aluminum is a daunting undertaking, and the most common method used today, known as the Hall-Heroult process, involves several steps that, by rights, should have been beyond the capabilities of the third-century Chinese. Among the complex procedures is the heating of an oxide of aluminum, extracted from bauxite ore, to a temperature of 970 degrees Celsius, and the subsequent passing of an electric current through the molten substance. No one knows what process the Chinese used or whether the fastener was the result of some freak accident during smelting. It may be that those ancient metalworkers were familiar with a technique that has since been lost.

Conceivably, the modern method may not have been out of their reach. How else can one explain such objects as specimens of Babylonian jewelry dating from the second millennium BC and exhibiting such delicate layering of metals that they appear to have been electroplated? Items of gold jewelry recovered from excavations near the Great Pyramid in Egypt by the nineteenth-century archaeologist Auguste Mariette are similarly baffling. Mariette, in describing his finds for a contemporary encyclopedia, unhesitat-

ingly averred that their "thinness and lightness make one believe they had been produced by electroplating." He went on to say that the technique had only recently come into industrial use in Europe.

Some scholars believe that an intriguing find made in 1936 may provide the explanations for these puzzling anachronisms: The discovery could indicate that electricity was mastered before the end of the first millennium BC. The evidence, which was dug from the ruins of an ancient village near Baghdad, Iraq, consists of an earthenware vase that held a tube fashioned out of soldered sheet copper. The tube was sealed at its bottom by a copper disk. The other end was plugged with asphalt, a substance found in natural deposits throughout the Middle East and widely traded in biblical times. Inside the tube and protruding through the plug was an iron rod.

For a time, the artifact was stored in the basement of the Iraqi State Museum and classified as some sort of pot. Then, in 1938, a German man employed as a researcher on the museum staff, Wilhelm König, envisioned another possible function: Using clay as a casing, its makers had constructed a simple battery. König noted that if the tube had been filled with an acid solution—probably acetic or citric acid, also readily available at the time—it would have produced electricity. And it probably was not the only one of its kind. König determined that a number of similar vessels had been uncovered in the region. Possibly they had been linked together by thin iron and copper rods for a greater output of power.

At the General Electric High Voltage Laboratory in Massachusetts shortly after World War II, researchers built models based on the Baghdad artifact. Their experiments showed that its configuration, which effectively mimes that of modern batteries, will generate up to one-half volt of current. Three decades later, a German Egyptologist named Arne Eggebrecht took the next logical step. He constructed a replica, filled the copper tube with grape juice, and harnessed the current to electroplate a small silver statue with gold. Whether the Baghdad object was actually used that way remains open to debate. Some scholars think that the vessel's function was much less sophisticated: Its purpose may have been simply to hold a cosmetic or a scroll.

In his book *Worlds Before Our Own,* Brad Steiger, author of numerous volumes on spiritualism and unexplained phenomena, lays out several interrelated theories elaborating on the supposition that the knowledge of electricity stood as one of the central mysteries of earlier civilizations. Rather than being widely disseminated, the know-how for its production resided in the hands of an elite cadre and was passed on only under the cloak of secrecy. This assumption, say Steiger and others, would make sense of numerous otherwise inexplicable archaeological findings—for instance, the fact that nowhere within the labyrinthine tunnels and chambers running throughout the pyramids of Egypt is there any sign of soot from torches. Yet the interiors could not have been illuminated by anything but artificial light, since they are windowless.

Such theories pose another question. Did the possessors of the principles of electricity derive their knowledge from research done in their own day, or was it a legacy from some earlier time? That same issue of inheritance is often raised on a much broader level. Agriculture, hydraulics, astronomy, law, writing, mathematics, and economics—all the defining characteristics of civilization burst quickly into bloom at numerous spots around the world within a relatively short span of time. This eruption of knowledge has nagged at many an imaginative mind. Unsatisfied that humankind could vault from supposed barbarity to sophistication almost overnight, these thinkers speculate that much of the knowledge explosion was in fact prompted by the advanced civilizations that allegedly thrived before the dawn of history.

These ancestral races have been painted, more often than not, as superior beings who scaled great intellectual heights and then were brought down by their own pride or by natural disasters of an unprecedented violence. Out of their wreckage grew the early cities of Eurasia and Africa and Mesoamerica—bequeathed a stupendous treasury of knowledge by fortunate members of the older races who managed to escape destruction and find their way to more primitive shores.

Many seekers after alternative truths believe that a description of the rise of a superior race of human beings is contained in the Old Testament. Rene Noorbergen, who often addresses biblical and paranormal themes, contends in his 1977 work, entitled *Secrets of the Lost Races*, that embedded within the Book of Genesis is the tale of a race undergoing an accelerated evolution into a highly technological society. The ten generations of patriarchs that are said to have included both Adam and Noah reached an advanced state of development comparable to that of the modern age, asserts Noorbergen.

With lightning speed—even considering that each generation was of Methuselan length, averaging about 850 years according to Scripture—the pre-Flood Hebrews gained profound understanding of the workings of the cosmos and were able to apply what they had learned, Noorbergen believes. That mainstream scholars fail to recognize the signs of this achievement is not terribly surprising, he explains, for sometimes the most high-tech instrumentation can have deceptive appearances. "For example," he writes, "a network of lines traced with special metal-containing ink on specially treated paper can serve as a receiver for electromagnetic waves; a copper tube can serve as a resonator in the production of high-frequency waves; and the surface of a diamond can even be made to contain an image of the pages of 100,000 average-sized books!" Bizarrely anachronistic artifacts that confound archaeologists now, Noorbergen adds, may become comprehensible "as we ourselves approach or reach the same stage of advancement" as antediluvian culture.

From the Bible also come indications that the antediluvian races cut a larger figure than did their puny descendants. Goliath, the giant who was felled by David, perhaps was one late member of an elder race. But the Old Testament is by no means alone in intimating that giants once strode the earth. Believers point out

According to some researchers, the minuscule holes in these tiny quartz beads, unearthed with a Peruvian mummy, suggest an inexplicably high level of technical skill for an ancient civilization. It was previously assumed that the tools necessary for such delicate drilling were fairly recent developments.

Leaving an inky row of storklike birds in its wake, this rolling device for printing, found amid ruins in the Andes, dates from about AD 1000. The birds bear a striking resemblance to Egyptian artwork of an earlier time.

that anecdotal evidence can be glimpsed in legends, myths, sacred writings, and folk tales from around the world. The list of alleged gigantic races includes the Titans, who were unseated by Zeus and his Olympian cohorts; the huge-bodied Allegewi tribe reputed by the Delaware and Sioux Indians to have occupied the Mississippi River region in the distant past; the Norse Frost Giants and Mountain Giants, who cut a swath through Jotunheim; and a legendary people of ancient China who were described as being "twice as tall as us." The accounts of these and other gargantuan beings are held to be distorted versions of ancient realities, garbled memories from the depths of time.

Beginning in the 1950s, Clifford Burdick, a popular author who built a reputation by disputing the standard Darwinian picture of evolution, contended that amateur archaeologists had unearthed ample signs of long-extinct races of giants. Burdick actively investigated the work of several hobbyists who claimed that they had discovered outsize fossil prints. Between 1938 and 1950, one amateur excavator, Jim Ryals of Texas, purportedly uncovered several sets of tracks from sediments along the banks of the Paluxy River southwest of Dallas. The most impressive prints measured sixteen inches long and eight inches wide. In photographs, a beaming Ryals displays casts of them alongside those of a three-toed dinosaur taken from impressions that shared the same stratum.

Although two-foot-long humanlike tracks have reportedly been found at isolated sites throughout Western deserts, few scientists accept that such prints represent genuine evidence of colossal beings, especially when claims are made that such creatures walked the earth during the age of dinosaurs, more than 65 million years ago. Paleontologists argue that the prints were either formed by giant ground sloths or, in some cases, faked.

Proponents of the race-of-giants hypothesis find other proofs in the fossil record, however. They cite, for example, reports (admittedly rather dated) alleging the existence of outsize skeletons in European gravesites. The Scottish fifteenth-century historian Hector Boece mentioned a fourteen-foot skeleton, and the bones of men who had stood even taller—up to thirty-three feet—reputedly came to light in Spain and at locations around southern Italy in the sixteenth and eighteenth centuries.

Remains of slightly less statuesque but nonetheless extraordinarily tall people have also been found in Mexico and Central America. In 1930, a mining engineer working along the Yaqui River in the Mexican state of Sonora became convinced that he had discovered an entire cemetery full of Brobdingnagian corpses. These, reported the *New York Times,* "averaging eight feet in height, were found buried tier by tier." It should be noted, however, that at least one distinguished expert on archaeology during that time, museum curator Bernard Brown, rejected the authenticity of the miner's claim and threw into doubt the validity of other similar stories. As Brown explained the problem, "First reports of the discovery of skeletons by persons unfamiliar with proper methods of measurement almost invariably exaggerate the height."

In the lore of lost races, one strain of thought has captured the imagination and credence of more people throughout the centuries than any other. Literally millions of words have been spent exploring and defending the concept that the lost race that endowed more-recent humans with the

Geologist Clifford Burdick displays a pair of petrified tracks from a Texas riverbed. He believes that the imprint on the left was made by a dinosaur and the one on the right by an enormous human. Burdick has deduced that the stride of such a giant "was about six feet until the fellow started to run, when the stride lengthened to nine feet."

fundaments of knowledge once dwelled in harmony and wealth on the island of Atlantis. The legend of a sunken nation in the Atlantic Ocean has drawn the attention of mystics and scholars alike.

Concerning the origins of this particular mythos, there can be no doubt: The fourth-century-BC Greek philosopher Plato was the first to mention the Atlanteans, who played the part of avatars of civilization in two dialogues, the *Timaeus* and the *Critias.* These were playlets, in effect—extended conversations that supposedly took place among a group of prominent men who had gathered in Athens seven decades earlier. In the dialogues, Plato attempts to establish the veracity of the Atlantis story by citing its provenance. The account, says one of the conversationalists, was "a story derived from ancient traditions." It had been handed down in his family since the time of his relative Solon, a seventh-century-BC Athenian statesman, who apparently heard it directly from an Egyptian priest.

Plato recounts that the Atlanteans lived in a magnificent circular city on an island lying in the ocean just beyond the Straits of Gibraltar. Sitting at the city's center was an acropolis upon which were built richly decorated palaces that looked down over a series of encircling canals and snug harbors; a sheltered passage led in from the sea. Beyond the city's limits, on the landward side, stretched a tilled plain irrigated by an intricate system of channels.

The Atlanteans were a glitteringly intelligent race, and they especially endeared themselves to Plato by their ideal political constitution—an agreement based on god-given laws, which called for the entire citizenry of the island to assemble once a year to settle disputes in an equitable fashion. In time, however, the islanders fell prey to imperialistic tendencies, and their overambitiousness triggered the wrath of the gods, who caused the idyllic land to be wracked by earthquakes, floods, and torrential rains, and finally to subside into the maw of the sea.

Plato's own pupil Aristotle said of Atlantis after his master's death, "He who invented it, also destroyed it," and other classical thinkers were similarly dismissive of the conceit. But medieval authors revived the story, and as a resource-hungry Europe began expanding into uncharted waters, the renown of the vanished island burgeoned. Sailors sought its shadowy outlines beneath the ocean's surface and brought back further news of ghostly landfalls that rose and fell beneath the sea at whim.

Speculation about a submerged civilization was fired by enigmatic references in the traditions of New World peoples. No less a scholar than Sir Francis Bacon—the seventeenth-century philosopher and author who is credited with laying the foundations of the scientific method—found it entirely reasonable to assume that the New World was in some way related to the continent of Atlantis. Another writer of the seventeenth century, John Swan, wrote in a volume called *Speculum Mundi:* "This I may think may be supposed, that America was sometimes part of that great land which Plato calleth the Atlantick island, and that the Kings of that island had some intercourse between the people of Europe and Africa."

Clues that would play an enormous role in the ultimate, nineteenth-century elaboration of the Atlantis tale were deduced from Mayan and Aztec traditions by two clerics, the Spanish bishop Diego de Landa, who accompanied the conquistadors to the New World, and his religious confrere, the French abbot Charles-Étienne Brasseur de Bourbourg, who traveled around Central America in the mid-nineteenth century.

De Landa, who was infamous among archaeologists for having burned all but three of the irreplaceable codices that had been kept by Mayan priests, in his later years developed a (perhaps perverse) interest in studying the customs and relics of the defeated Indian cultures. In a report to his Spanish peers, de Landa wrote: "Some of the old people of Yucatán say that they have heard from their ancestors that this land was occupied by a race of people, who came from the East and whom God had delivered by opening twelve paths through the sea." De Landa himself concluded that these people from the East were none other than the ten lost tribes of Israel, who had been banished from their homeland by Assyrian overlords in 700 BC and thence disappeared from history.

De Landa essayed to translate the Mayan alphabet, and although his crude effort has not held up to modern scrutiny, it was perceived as accurate in his day. In 1864, the Frenchman Brasseur found it quite adequate for the task of interpreting one of the surviving Mayan codices. According to Brasseur, the text contained a description of a catastrophe in which an island nation called Mu sank in similar fashion to Plato's Atlantis.

The unresolved musings of de Landa and Brasseur were taken up in turn by Ignatius T. Donnelly, arguably the most widely heeded proponent of a lost-race theory ever to live. Lawyer, editor, former U.S. Congressman, and a serious but misguided antiquary, Donnelly published his densely researched *Atlantis: The Antediluvian World* in 1882. It became an immediate bestseller and proved to have lasting popularity with readers, passing through fifty printings by the middle of the following century. So that there could be no mistake about his bias, Donnelly laid out his assumptions right on page one, asserting that Atlantis was "the true Antediluvian world; the Garden of Eden; the Garden of the Hesperides; the Elysian fields; the Gardens of Alcinous;

the Mesomphalos; the Mount Olympos; the Asgard; the focus of the traditions of the ancient nations; representing a universal memory of a great land, where early mankind dwelt for ages in peace and happiness."

Donnelly used the following 325 pages to fill in the details and to trace the spreading of the Atlantean legacy throughout the world. The work of both de Landa and Brasseur was invoked as documentation for the claim that the pre-Columbian peoples of Mexico had contact with Atlantis. This was the significance of the Mayan and Aztec legends that spoke of strangers who arrived from or sailed off toward the East.

Donnelly similarly found what was, to him, indisputable proof of "intercourse with Atlantis" in the records of practically every culture of the ancient world: Mayan, Aztec, Inca, Greek, Phoenician, Arabian, Egyptian, Semitic, Aryan, Ibero-Celtic, Native American. Without doubt, Donnelly wrote, the Atlanteans "were the founders of nearly all our arts and sciences; they were the parents of our fundamental beliefs; they were the first civilizers, the first navigators, the first merchants, the first colonizers of the earth; their civilization was old when Egypt was young, and they had passed away thousands of years before Babylon, Rome, or London were dreamed of. This lost people were our ancestors, their blood flows in our veins. Every line of race and thought, of blood and belief, leads back to them."

Donnelly's stimulating notions caught the eye of a less scrupulous student of prehistory, Madame Helena Petrovna Blavatsky, whose fame today far outstrips Donnelly's, in part because of her popularity among British and American literary circles of her day. A former circus bareback rider, pianist, spiritualist medium, and sweatshop worker, Blavatsky was a Russian native who had led a gypsy existence before settling in the United States. She gained widespread attention in 1888 with publication of her chief work, *The Secret Doctrine.*

In penning her magnum opus, Blavatsky mined her experiences in India, where she claimed to have obtained access to the *Stanzas of Dzyan,* an Atlantean tome that had been transported from the doomed island and preserved by farseeing holy men. This work of spiritual and cosmological clarity, Blavatsky claimed, charted the seven stages of life on earth, of which only the last two stages remain to be experienced. Over each stage, a dominant Root Race has held sway. The Atlanteans constituted the Fourth Root Race, and although they made notable achievements, they did not measure up to their predecessors, a people called the Lemurians.

There are numerous views on the Lemurians *(pages 6-15).* Ideas on the subject are so diverse, in fact, that Madame Blavatsky and her followers could not agree on the story among themselves. For her part, the grande dame of the occult believed that the civilization was the most spiritually advanced ever to have graced the planet. Its beginning was most peculiar, however. The Lemurians commenced their reign on earth as giant, apelike creatures with a third eye on the back of their heads. Over time, they evolved to more closely resemble humans. They had no written language, since they communicated telepathically. They also engaged in telekinesis, levitating objects at will. They were taught to control fire by visitors from Venus, who also instructed them in weaving, metallurgy, and agriculture. Lemuria, like Atlantis, suffered the fate of disappearing beneath the waves.

Interestingly, although Blavatsky concocted her accounts out of whole cloth (as well as by borrowing liberally from Donnelly, from contemporary translations of Hindu texts, and from other unacknowledged sources), the lost continent of Lemuria was actually the spawn of genuine scientific ponderings, which Blavatsky appropriated and distorted. Eager to bolster the evolutionary theory of Charles Darwin, certain nineteenth-century biologists had studied the question of how the arboreal mammals called lemurs could exist in almost identical form in both Madagascar, just off the east coast of Africa, and thousands of miles away in India. An English zoologist, Philip Schlater, postulated that Africa and India had once been part of a

contiguous landmass, which he dubbed, naturally enough, Lemuria. German naturalist Ernst Heinrich Haeckel shared Schlater's view and further asserted that Lemuria had been humankind's primeval home.

Scientists now know that the Indian landmass did once belong to Africa but that it broke off many millions of years ago and slowly sailed northeastward on the tectonic plates of the earth's crust until it crashed into Asia. Even without this modern understanding, however, the notion of the lost continent of Lemuria seemed quite plausible and was endorsed by many leading scientists of Schlater's day, including Alfred Russel Wallace, who had formulated the theory of natural selection independently of Darwin, and the zoologist Thomas Henry Huxley, nicknamed Darwin's Bulldog because of his ardent championing of the elder scientist's theory.

Again and again in the various visions of lost civilizations, the related themes of flight, levitation, and space travel have come up. In the 1950s, after examining stone structures built high in the Andes by the Incas centuries ago, Morris Jessup, an American astronomer-cum-explorer, came to the conclusion that mere muscle could never have moved the huge building blocks into place.

Jessup favored the hypothesis that spacemen armed with gravitationally powered "accelerators or lifting forces" had come to the aid of the Inca crews. The possibility of alien assistance for human projects was seconded by the French author Robert Charroux. Before his death in 1978, Charroux, who cast himself as a seeker of truth probing the "Mysterious Unknown," disseminated the view that the crowning glories of the Mexican, Egyptian, Phoenician, Sumerian, and Persian civilizations were owed to the skills of extraterrestrials, who obviously had the capability of transporting themselves within the atmosphere of earth and into space beyond. Charroux, whose writings displayed Blavatskian brio, had a pretty good idea of where these helpers were coming from: "Tradition maintains that they were Venusians."

Biblical descriptions of the prophet Elijah in his "fiery chariot," angels descending from the heavens enrobed in flame and cloud, and the bodily ascensions of Jesus and Mary have all been treated by maverick thinkers as literal accounts of events mediated by extraterrestrials. Proponents of the notion that early humans had close encounters with aliens find support for their view in certain ambiguous graphic representations *(pages 35-43)*. One example is an Australian rock drawing that portrays four figures wearing long robes and fitted with blue halos; these images bear inscriptions in an unknown language—taken by some stu-

Hardy Remnants of Ancient Races

For at least 5,000 years, the nomadic people known as the Lapps have lived in the vast Arctic wastes between the western coast of Norway and Russia's Kola Peninsula. The origins of this ancient people, whose physical appearance differs markedly from that of other Europeans, have long intrigued scholars. Modern research suggests that they may be an independent race, perhaps the original inhabitants of Europe, who were pushed northward by Indo-European invaders. Intensely traditional, they clung to their migratory ways, dwelling in tents and herding reindeer, until recent times. Of the 50,000 Lapps in the region today, however, most live in permanent communities.

A fair-skinned people of Caucasian appearance, the Ainu have inhabited the northernmost islands of Japan since time immemorial. They pose an anthropological enigma: Surrounded by Mongoloid peoples, they live thousands of miles from their nearest possible racial cousin. Moreover, the legends of this mysterious people, who resist modern ways and now number only a few thousand, offer no clues to their origins. Even their language is unique. Recent theories suggest that the Ainu, long scorned by the dominant racial group in Japan, may in fact be the true descendants of the vanished race called the Jomon. If so, they can claim as their forebears the original inhabitants of Japan.

proud and independent Basques have occupied the land they call
[Eus]kal-Herria for at least 5,000 years—and perhaps for as much as
[fif]teen times that long. Some scholars believe they were the original
[inha]bitants of the Iberian Peninsula. Their homeland comprises the
[wes]tern Pyrenees and nearby coastal regions of France and Spain.
[The] Basques are a distinct race, unrelated to other European blood-
[line]s. Like the Ainu, their language is entirely original. They are also
[disti]nguished by the world's highest incidence of Rh-negative blood.
[Afte]r centuries of self-imposed isolation, many Basque villagers value
[thei]r uniqueness and cling to simple lives as farmers and fishers.

Long the focus of romantic fascination as well as of contempt and
prejudice, the Gypsies originated in northern India. By the 1400s,
bands of the exotic travelers were wandering all over Europe. Some
claimed to be religious pilgrims from a place called Little Egypt; this
explains their English name, which is short for Egyptians. By modern
times, Gypsies had spread around the world. Despite their extensive
dispersion, however, they remain remarkably distinct in their ethnic
identity. Indeed, it has been by clinging to their nomadic ways—albeit
with mobile homes nowadays more often than with horse-drawn wag-
ons—that the Gypsies have resisted assimilation by other cultures.

dents of mysterious phenomena to be primitive renderings of visitors from space. The local Aborigines support this interpretation, saying that the drawings illustrate the first men and were made by "another race." According to Aboriginal belief, both technology and their own folk medicine derived from the teachings of these men.

In recent years, the most widely read treatment of an ancient aeronautical theme was *Chariots of the Gods?,* by the Swiss author Erich von Däniken. A zealous, self-taught student of archaeology, von Däniken claimed in print and later in a television production based on his book that a Mayan rock carving shows an ancient astronaut strapped into his capsule as the rocket below roars into action to lift him into outer space. Von Däniken and others also argue that massive earthworks, such as the animal and insect figures carved out of the chalky Nazca Plain in Peru, are proof that early peoples had some means for rising above the terrain, since these vast images can be viewed in their entirety only from the air.

Some of the writers who espouse such theories even claim to know what sort of aircraft were used in the forgotten ages of humankind. In the 1970s, a team of researchers (including a NASA engineer) examined a gold pendant discovered in a precinct of northern Colombia and decided that it mimed a jet aircraft, down to its snub nose, delta wing, and vertical stabilizer. Critics charged that the resemblance was superficial and that the pendant more likely was a sculpted version of the devilfish, a common member of the ray family, which is today dried and sold in traditional Central and South American outdoor markets.

Another supposed indicator of ancient flight is Egyptian in origin. In 1969, Egyptologist Khalil Messiha came across a long-ignored artifact—a small object resembling a model of a glider—that was gathering dust in the basement of the Cairo Museum of Antiquities. Records revealed that it had been found in a 2,100-year-old tomb near Saqqara in 1898. Made of lightweight sycamore wood, it had straight wings, a streamlined body, and a vertical tail fin. A flick of the wrist was sufficient to send it sailing gracefully through the air. But perhaps gliding flight was only part of what it had originally modeled. Apparently something had broken off the lower part of the tail—which suggested to some investigators that the model had once included an engine. On the other hand, the artifact could simply have been a toy or a weather vane rather than a miniature version of an ancient airplane.

Travel by plane is discussed in considerable detail in several ancient Sanskrit texts, including the Yajur-Veda, the Ramayana, and the Mahabharata, a 200,000-line epic poem set down in the fourth or fifth century BC. In the Mahabharata, heroes traverse the heavens in winged "celestial cars" or "aerial chariots" clad in iron. In an eleventh-century compilation of earlier texts, this summary description of flight is given: "The aircraft which can go by its own force like a bird—on the earth or water or through the air—is called a Vimana. That which can travel in the sky from place to place is called a Vimana by the sages of old. The body must be strong and durable and shaped like a bird in flight with wings outstretched. Within it must be placed the mercury engine, with its heating apparatus made of iron underneath. When these are heated by controlled fire from under the iron containers, the Vimana possesses thunder power through the mercury. The iron engine must have properly welded joints to be filled with mercury, and when fire is conducted to the upper part, it develops power with the roar of a lion."

These same Hindu texts chronicle the downfall of the sages of old. The Vimanas, it seems, were used to wage war against other advanced peoples. The Mahabharata tells of dark days when vying factions of the races living in the upper Ganges region obliterated one another using the "Agneya weapon," an agent of awesome destructive force launched from marauding Vimanas. The epic recounts that in one sortie, a Vimana released a "blazing missile of smokeless fire." Immediately, "dense arrows of flame, like a great shower, issued forth upon creation, encompassing the enemy. Meteors flashed down from the sky. A thick gloom swiftly settled upon the Pandava hosts. All points of the compass were lost in darkness. Fierce winds began to blow. Clouds roared upward, showering dust and gravel." The landscape was strafed by fire, and animals as well as people were cut down with no hope of escape. Corpses were charred beyond recognition.

To some readers, this description evokes the harrowing narratives of survivors of the atomic-bomb blasts at Hiroshima and Nagasaki. In fact, it is sometimes argued that buried within the collective consciousness of humankind is the repressed memory of a trauma of cosmic proportions, a memory of planetwide destruction in an all-nuclear war. As evidence, believers point to the ruins of numerous ancient strongholds that supposedly bear signs of a horrific end game played out by forgotten superpowers. Certain fortresses along the banks of the Ganges appear to have been subjected to intense heat; in places, the walls have a glazed appearance, as if turned partly to glass. The same feature turns up on ziggurats in Babylon. At a site in Israel, archaeologists' trenches revealed a strange greenish layer some sixteen feet deep in the desert; the layer consisted of vitrified sand, similar to that produced in the aftermath of the first aboveground tests of nuclear warheads in Nevada in the 1950s.

A team of Soviet authors, Valentin Rich and Mikhail Chernenkov, suggested in 1960 that the story of the destruction of Sodom and Gomorrah embodied the essential truth of a nuclear holocaust that took place in an earlier time. However, the catastrophe that struck the sin-laced

twin cities need not have been as exotic as one might suppose. Even in 100 BC, the Greek historian Strabo was commenting on the geologic instability of the region, where the land was frequently wracked by earthquakes and overrun by bubbling streams of asphalt that percolated up from underground in that petroleum-rich zone. Erich von Däniken, for one, is convinced that exchanges of a nuclear nature took place in distant times. "Here as there," he writes in surveying two sites of unnatural-looking devastation, "one is forcibly given the impression of an explosive destruction, an annihilation that cannot be attributed to the passage of thousands of years, a chaos that could not have been created without an explosion on the Hiroshima scale."

A countervailing school of thought maintains that the superior civilizations of prehistory perished not by fire but by water. Flood legends can be found in the literature and lore of peoples throughout the world. Tales of cataclysmic deluges that destroyed all of humanity except for a few virtuous souls were or are recounted by the indigenous inhabitants of Wales, Persia, India, Australia, and the South Seas. In addition, the Norse, the Lithuanians, the Inuit, the Apache, and the Indonesians each have their own version of the story.

The archetypal flood story occurs in the biblical Book of Genesis. Proponents such as the contemporary author Rene Noorbergen contend that the Genesis account gives an accurate rendering of a long-ago calamity. Whether or not this is true, it is a powerful tale: After the rise of the antediluvian patriarchs, human beings fall into evil ways. An angry God decides to wipe the slate clean, saving only Noah and his family, who are directed to build a vessel that will carry them and the beasts of the world to safety. Genesis recounts that on the very day Noah discharged his carpentering duty "were all the fountains of the great deep broken up . . . and the waters prevailed exceedingly upon the earth, and all the high hills were covered." Landing safely on Mount Ararat once the waters receded, Noah is told by God to do his best to reconstruct society. After a brief, peaceful interregnum, an attempt is made to bring together all of Noah's descendants at the Tower of Babel and to give them a common language, but this effort fails miserably, and humanity is scattered to the four corners of the globe in virtual chaos.

The ancient Babylonian Epic of Gilgamesh also contains a flood story, and it bears a significant resemblance to the Hebraic version. In this epic, the Babylonian patriarch Utnapishtim, like Noah, receives warning of an imminent flood in which all humanity will die. He builds a boat and sails to safety with his family, taking along assorted artisans and a number of animals. After a tumultuous seven-day storm, Utnapishtim successively sends out three birds in search of land—a dove, a swallow, and a raven. When the raven does not return, he makes the decision to debark on Mount Nisir.

Those who argue that a planetary flood actually occurred see in the common features of the flood myths confirmation that each story derived ultimately from a single account of the tribulation—that of Noah and his family—which was carried around the world with the dispersal of peoples from the Tower of Babel. Noorbergen finds prima facie evidence of this in Chinese tradition, which holds that the progenitor of the Chinese race was a man named Nu-wah, who managed to escape an all-encompassing flood with his wife and children.

Russian scholar Immanuel Velikovsky in 1955 further maintained that the fossil record supports the contention that the planet once underwent wholesale inundation as described in myth and Scripture. "Entire shoals of fish over large areas, numbering billions of specimens, are found in a state of agony, but with no mark of a scavenger's attack," he wrote. But Velikovsky had his own peculiar view of what

constituted divine intervention. The worldwide deluge, he argued, had resulted when the forerunner of the planet Venus—then a comet that had been spewn from the bowels of the planet Jupiter—sailed close to Earth, knocking it off its previous axis and causing rivers, lakes, and oceans to slosh around like so much bathwater.

Sincere as they may be in their efforts to decipher the riddles of the past, flood theorists have a limited understanding of the geologic record. Although a layperson who finds fossils of oceanic creatures on a mountaintop might draw the ancient high-water mark there, geologists are certain that within the last 100,000 years the sea has not lapped more than 100 feet above its present level. And probably never in the earth's 4.5-billion-year existence has it been completely submerged in water. Moreover, as nearly as can be determined within the limits of the science of meteorology, it is simply not possible that torrential rains could ever have flooded simultaneously all the low-lying portions of the planet.

But geologists can offer at least a measure of solace to those who desire to read in ancient texts signs of common heritage. Sediments distributed throughout the Tigris and Euphrates basin—the setting for the Epic of Gilgamesh, and the land of exile for the Jews from 598 to 515 BC—indicate that a flood of mighty proportions occurred there sometime during the fourth millennium before the birth of Christ. It may well be that the water's rise came slowly enough so that the peoples who had settled in this fertile region were able to gather their meager belongings together, to grab a few last sheaves of wheat from the fields, and to hustle their few scrawny goats and pigs and cows north toward higher ground. As they made the arduous journey, robbed of certainty and not yet buoyed by hope, perhaps one among them began silently composing the story of a man and his family and his animals cast upon the waters and bound for new lands, a story that he would share with his companions that night and for many nights to come as they passed the time around the fire.

A Theory of Astral Ancestry

Prehistory as we have learned it," wrote British anthropologist and archaeologist Colin Renfrew, "is based upon several assumptions which can no longer be accepted as valid." One such assumption—about the origin of humans—has always been an area of contradiction and confusion. For many, neither the theory of evolution nor the biblical story of creation satisfactorily explains the birth of humanity. The answer, some nontraditional thinkers suggest: ancient astronauts.

Traditional science proposes that severe climatic changes account for the spasmodic progression of our primitive ancestors into more advanced people, but those who subscribe to the idea of alien forebears speculate that in the distant past, beings from a faraway solar system visited earth, interbreeding with—or genetically manipulating—the existing anthropoid population to raise it to a higher plane. As proof of this theory, they cite gaps in archaeological evidence of the physical evolution of humankind and argue that outside forces must have shaped human development.

Evidence of extraterrestrial intervention, proponents assert, can be found in prehistoric rock carvings and paintings such as the one above and those on the next eight pages. Believers claim these works depict ancient astronauts either seen by the artists or learned of through oral tradition. Conventional scholars concede that some of the depictions resemble figures in spacesuits and helmets. But they hold that while the images do indeed reflect myste-

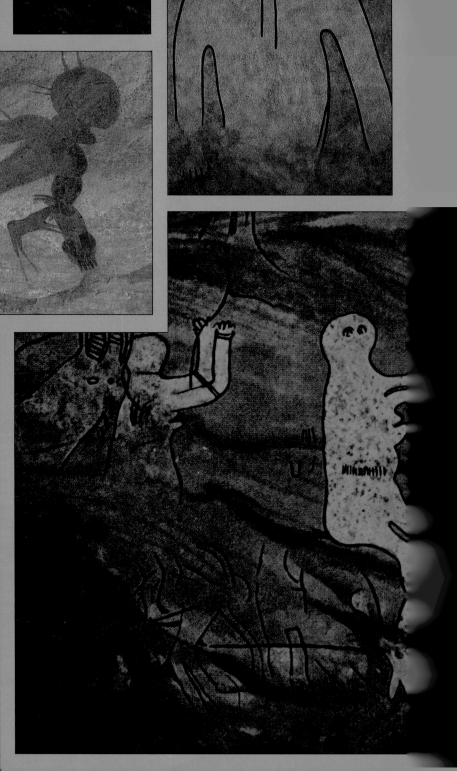

Cave Art and the Extraterrestrial

Not until humans developed space technology, say proponents of the ancient-astronaut theory, could prehistoric rock paintings such as the ones shown here—believed to date from 8000 to 6000 BC—be recognized as records of alien encounters. Henri Lhote, who discovered many frescoes in the central Sahara in 1956, dubbed one painting (above right) the Great Martian God because it resembled fanciful pictures he had seen of Martians. Believers say the figure's round head and peculiar features reveal it to be a helmeted space alien, an identity also ascribed to the creature in the fresco above, called The Swimmer. The painting at right, Great God with Praying Women, supposedly also depicts extraterrestrials, although most scholars believe it represents a fertility cult.

On a rock face in northern Australia—almost half a world away from the similar Saharan pictures—primitive drawings such as the one above have been interpreted as prehistoric astronauts clad in zippered spacesuits and antenna-topped helmets. Paintings of the haunting, mouthless creatures known as wandjina (right) have also been viewed as depicting space aliens who visited Australia in earlier times, although native tradition holds they are spirits who bring water to the arid region. Local Aborigines insist the pictures—some of which may be as old as 5,000 years—are the work of the otherworldly beings they portray.

Halos or
Space Headgear?

On Australia's Nourlangie Rock, a prehistoric line of tall, haloed figures with cross-hatched bodies stands next to a crouching creature (right). Although the halo has long been a symbol of sacredness and importance, those who believe in ancient astronauts claim that it resembles headgear—as in the 500 BC Italian rock carving above—or symbolizes one who came from the skies.

The similarity of ray-emanating figures in these prehistoric petroglyphs from California (below), Peru (at right below), and the Soviet Union (near right) has convinced some that extraterrestrial intervention was a worldwide phenomenon.

The radial design in this New Zealand rock painting links it with other far-distant images (left), said to symbolize ancient aliens.

CHAPTER 2

Mystical Monarchies

atherine Maltwood thought the lodging she took in the Somerset village of Glastonbury in the summer of 1929 would be temporary. She had an artist's commission for a newly translated version of *Le haut livre du Graal,* or *The High History of the Holy Graal,* an ancient text that described the adventures of King Arthur and his knights. The book's original Latin manuscript was purported to have been written at Glastonbury Abbey, once considered the most sacred church in England and the legendary burial site of Arthur. Maltwood's purpose in visiting Glastonbury was to search out landmarks where the Arthurian legends might have occurred and then to use those landmarks in designing a map for the book.

Roaming the fields and ruins in and around Glastonbury, Maltwood felt certain that she recognized many of the sites described in *The High History of the Holy Graal.* But she also began to be haunted: Something else lay hidden in the landscape, some pattern that she could not quite make out. Maltwood went about her work troubled by the feeling that some essential aspect of the local countryside was barely eluding her.

Then, one warm, clear evening, as she stood gazing from a rise on the edge of the village toward the legendary site of King Arthur's castle on Cadbury Hill, eleven miles to the southeast, Maltwood discerned what seemed to be two giant effigies formed by landscape features in the countryside below: One was of a lion, the other of a seated, human-looking creature. The shapes of the figures were evoked by combinations of hills, earthworks, roads, ancient field boundaries, and natural and man-made waterways. Later, she described them to an acquaintance who happened to be an astrologer, and this person suggested they might be Leo and one of the Gemini twins of the zodiac. Maltwood suddenly realized she had discovered a long-kept secret of the Glastonbury landscape.

Working from maps and aerial photographs that she had commissioned, she identified an entire vast circle of such colossal images, a ring more than ten miles in diameter that she believed accurately represented the twelve signs of the zodiac—in correct order from Aries to Pisces. Just outside the circle was a thirteenth image, that of the great dog Langport, who, according to Celtic folklore, guards the entrance to Annwn, the underworld home of the fairies.

Maltwood gave up her career in art and devoted the rest of her life to the study of her terrestrial zodiac. She concluded that the ancient people of Somerset had embellished nature's existing shapes and outlines some 5,000 years ago to create the zodiacal figures, and that in later centuries the monks of Glastonbury Abbey had carefully—and secretly—preserved the landmarks that gave form to the enormous figures.

Although she apparently never knew it, Katherine Maltwood was not the first person to see celestial giants in the Somerset countryside. Some 350 years earlier, John Dee, a man of many talents who had wielded influence in the fields of science, philosophy, mathematics, and alchemy, had also become entranced with Glastonbury's unusual topographic markings and had concluded, as Maltwood would later, that the twelve signs of the zodiac had been purposefully laid out in the landscape by an ancient and intelligent people.

For a short time, Dee's opinions in matters relating to the stars were of considerable importance, because he functioned as an astrological adviser to Queen Elizabeth I. "Thus is astrologie and astronomie carefullie and exactley married and measured in a scientific reconstruction of the heavens which shews that the ancients understode all which today the lerned know to be factes," Dee wrote. For Malt-

wood, though, the Glastonbury zodiac had more than astrological or archaeological significance. She believed that the existence of the figures explained many references found in old legends about King Arthur. "It is around these archaic nature giants that the Arthurian legends accumulated," she wrote. She saw the zodiac as the original Round Table: Arthur, for example, was Sagittarius, Guinevere was Virgo, Sir Lancelot was Leo, and Merlin was Capricorn.

Maltwood published her discovery of the Glastonbury zodiac in 1935. The book, titled *A Guide to Glastonbury's Temple of the Stars,* caused an immediate stir in England. Some people were so captivated by the notion of magic symbols etched in the earth that they joined her in her work. Others described her findings as fanciful nonsense, arguing that if any mammoth forms could be discerned in the Glastonbury landscape they were simply a coincidence of nature. Maltwood died in 1961, her work still revered by a few enthusiasts but largely forgotten.

The Glastonbury zodiac, whether real or imagined, is one of many reflections of the mysterious, ever-receding, visionary realm of King Arthur. The exact location of his kingdom—indeed, its very existence—has long been debated by historians, archaeologists, and dreamers. But the legend of this romantic idealist with his brave (and mostly loyal) knights, his magical sword, and his beautiful queen, Guinevere, has become deeply rooted in British folklore, particularly in southwestern England. So immense is Great Britain's collective memory of King Arthur that it may be said that

Aquarius
(phoenix)

Pisces

Aries

Taurus

Cancer
(boat)

Gemini

Leo

Ca

Sagitta

Scorpio

Libra
(dove)

Virgo

*British artist Katherine Maltwood (bottom)
pauses during work on a sculpture. In 192
some twenty years after the photograph wc
taken, Maltwood discovered what she calle
the Temple of the Stars (top), an ancient
zodiacal chart embedded in the topography
of Somerset, England. The twelve symbols
illustrated here in shades of gray—cover
nearly eighty square miles, incorporating
natural features of the terrain as well as
roads, waterways, and earthworks. Open,
flat countryside, for instance, gives way to
dense forest, rugged hills, and steep gorges
forming the head and mane of the lion
that is the zodiacal symbol for Leo (center)*

46

the wise and benevolent warrior-monarch is still the island's most revered hero.

Historical proof of other mystical monarchies, such as the fabulous African (or Arabian) kingdom of Ophir, where the Bible says King Solomon obtained his gold, and the powerful and pious Asian realm of the Christian priest-emperor Prester John, has also eluded scholars. Yet tales of these lost kingdoms, like those of Arthur and his royal court, persist to this day. There is something in them that invites belief, in spite of naysayers' cold logic. As a result, elusive legend and hard history still contend for acceptance in these matters, as they have for centuries. The struggle to unravel fact from fiction draws some investigators into a pursuit as confounding as any quest for the Holy Grail or the secrets of the alchemists. The search has, in the past, led a few historians to undertake difficult journeys to far-off lands and—in at least one celebrated case—to foray into the realm of the spirits. What all the researchers find, without question, are stirring accounts of wonder and achievement.

Of all the fabled realms, none has so engaged the imagination of Western humanity as that of King Arthur and his goodly land of Camelot. Arthur may have slain evil giants, fiery dragons, and other monstrous beasts, but it was his war against oppression, aided by a mixture of prowess and virtue, that makes people long for the return of such a monarch. If heaven is unattainable for the time being, then Camelot will do.

In the search for Arthur's lost kingdom, historians have assiduously combed the meager written record of the legendary ruler. Although Arthur is said to have lived during the sixth century, no surviving documents of that time even mention his name. The earliest known reference to Arthur came 300 years later in a book titled *Historia Britonum (History of the Britons)*. Written in Latin by a Welsh cleric named Nennius, the book is a chaotic hodgepodge of old Celtic stories, some of them adapted from documents that have long since disappeared. Nennius introduced Arthur not as a king but as a heroic warrior—probably a great general. "Arthur

fought against the Saxons alongside the kings of the Britons, but he himself was the leader in the battles," Nennius wrote. He went on to describe the sites of Arthur's many battles, including one at Mount Badon, where Arthur reportedly slew 960 men single-handedly. None of these battle sites has been firmly identified. Nennius also reported that Arthur had a son named Anir, whom the great warrior himself killed and buried.

Nennius ended his *Historia* with an appendix of "Mirabilia," or "Marvels," including two involving Arthur. One entry described how the tomb of Arthur's son changed dimensions each time it was measured. "Whatever length you find it at one time you will find it different at another, and I myself have proved this to be true," he wrote. Nennius also told of a stack of stones that Arthur had piled together in southern Wales. The top stone bore the paw print of Arthur's dog, Cabal. "And men will come and carry away that stone for a day and a night, and the next morning there it is back again on its heap," wrote Nennius. These two tales, as well as the story of Arthur's superhuman slaughter of his enemies at Mount Badon, reveal the beginnings of the myth-making process that would continue to glorify the figure of Arthur even to this day.

Two other important early references to Arthur can be found in the *Annales Cambriae (Annals of Wales)*, a tenth-century Latin manuscript listing 533 years of wars, coronations, and other historical events. Mention is made of Arthur at the battle of Mount Badon, where he is said to have worn the "cross of Our Lord Jesus Christ on his shoulders for three days and three nights and the Britons were victors." A second entry cites Arthur's death at the battle of Camlan around 540. "Medrawt"—undoubtedly the traitorous Mordred of later legend—is also said to have died at Camlan, although the *Annales* do not declare whether he was Arthur's friend or foe.

These early written records provide only the sketchiest of profiles. Arthur was apparently born near the end of the fifth century. Meager evidence suggests a few other assertions that have come to be generally accepted by historians: Arthur's family was either of direct Roman descent or of aristocratic Celtic stock with close ties to the Romans. He was not a king but a valiant soldier who successfully led the Britons against the invading Saxons in a number of battles. He perished on the battlefield around the year 540, not at the hands of the Saxons but probably as the result of a family quarrel.

Barring the possibility that the legends of royalty were in fact correct—and that all traces of Arthur's kingship have simply been lost to history—it appears that a storied war hero was the beneficiary of a vastly expanded reputation. As the centuries passed, Arthur was promoted from battle commander to king and ranked with Alexander the Great and Charlemagne as one of the greatest military leaders of medieval Europe. He was rarely described in unfavorable terms, usually as a wise and noble monarch who, after successfully conquering his enemies, reigned over his domain in peace and prosperity for many years.

The first book to outline the grander view of Arthur was the *Historia regum Britanniae,* or *History of the Kings of Britain,* considered by some historians to be one of the most important manuscripts of the Middle Ages. Completed around 1136, the *Historia* was written by Geoffrey of Monmouth, a cleric and teacher at Oxford. Geoffrey claimed to have used as his source a "certain very ancient book in the British language," although no trace of this seminal and mysterious volume survives, and some scholars doubt that it ever existed. Geoffrey's account of Arthur is probably the culmination of 600 years of tales handed down from generation to generation by English, Irish, Welsh, and French storytellers. To top it off, Geoffrey added some fairly elaborate embellishments of his own.

The *Historia* introduced Merlin, arguably the most fabled magician of all time. In one account, Merlin made the megaliths of Stonehenge fly from Ireland to England's Salisbury Plain. Geoffrey also told how Merlin arranged for Uther Pendragon—in ancient Britain, a pendragon was preeminent among many kings—to go to Igraine, the beautiful duchess of Cornwall, in the guise of her husband. The liaison left the duchess pregnant with Arthur. Geoffrey went on to describe how Arthur became king at the age of fifteen years, wielded a sword called Caliburn (Excalibur in later versions of the story), and not only routed the Saxons from Britain but conquered much of Europe.

Having, in Geoffrey's words, "restored Britain to its earlier dignity," Arthur married Guinevere and established a great medieval court. Eventually, however, he was betrayed by his nephew Mordred, who conspired with the Saxons and declared himself king while Arthur was abroad. Arthur defeated Mordred in a series of battles but was grievously wounded. His loyal knights carried him to the Isle of Avalon, where they were met by Morgan le Fay, a benevolent enchantress. "She put the king in her chamber on a golden bed, uncovered his wound with her noble hand and looked long at it," Geoffrey wrote. "At length she said he could be cured if only he stayed with her a long while and accepted her treatment." Not surprisingly, Arthur agreed to her terms.

Thus, Geoffrey put his imprimatur on the traditional belief that Arthur did not die from his battle wounds but still lives on some mysterious, magical island. From there, it is said, he will return one day to help the Celtic people regain sovereignty over their land.

Arthur's story received its fullest and most detailed rendering in the fifteenth century at the pen of Sir Thomas Malory, a man who had more in common with the villains in the Arthurian legends than with the heroes. Malory was born around 1416 to a wealthy and respected English family. As a young man he apparently thieved, extorted, raped, and murdered. He went to prison eight times and escaped twice—once, reportedly, by swimming across a moat in full battle armor. Despite his unchivalrous behavior, Malory was a great admirer of the Arthurian romances. During one of his imprisonments, he wrote what he described as "the whole book of King Arthur and his noble knights of the Round Table." Malory's publisher renamed the work *Le Morte d'Arthur.*

The author selected the tales for his book from both French and English sources, arranging them in a coherent sequence. He attached to the Arthurian legend two of the most popular romances of the Middle Ages—the great love story of Tristan and Isolde and the quest for the Holy Grail. He also firmly established the central cast of characters around which all future Arthurian tales would revolve—the noble King Arthur, the beautiful Queen Guinevere, her lover Sir Lancelot, the wizard Merlin, the valiant knights Gareth and Gawain, and the traitorous Mordred.

Quite apart from his role in popularizing Arthurian legend, Malory proved to be an important figure in the development of English literature in general. The source of this broader influence was the author's decision not to render *Le Morte d'Arthur* in verse. In this, he was running contrary to long-established practice in the writing of epic tales. Malory's book has been cited by many literary historians as one of the earliest and most significant foundations of English prose tradition.

Some scholars believe that glorified stories of the real Arthur, the warrior who led his troops to victory against the Saxons, became blended with ancient stories of Celtic gods to create the great Arthurian legends. Both the names and personalities of Gawain and Lancelot, for example, have been traced to Celtic sun gods. In addition, many of the tales told of Arthur were once told of the Celtic god Gwy-

dion. Like Gwydion, Arthur brought culture and art to his people and was forced to wage war to ensure that his kingdom did not fall under the heels of marauding barbarians. Both Arthur and Gwydion attempted to steal swine from the keepers of the underworld; Gwydion succeeded, while Arthur did not. And both were captured and imprisoned for a time in Hades.

Many different sites throughout Britain, each with its own tales of strange and supernatural happenings, have become associated with Arthur. Geoffrey of Monmouth set Arthur's birthplace at Tintagel Castle on the rugged Cornish coast of southwestern England. Skeptics point out that the castle at this location was built in the twelfth century, much too late for Arthur's birth. However, archaeological excavations on the craggy headlands near the castle ruins have revealed the remains of other stone buildings, perhaps belonging to a Celtic monastery or to the home fortress of a wealthy Cornish family. Fragments of Mediterranean pottery from the fifth and sixth centuries have been found in these excavations, which would date the site to around the time of Arthur—and help to explain Geoffrey's logic in setting Arthur's birth there.

The Cornish people have named two rock formations near Tintagel Castle Arthur's Chair and Arthur's Cups and

King Arthur stands victorious over the crowns of thirty vanquished realms in this illustration from a fourteenth-century manuscript. The image of Mary and Jesus on his shield was said to have fortified him during his many conquests.

An Obsession with the Human Head

More than a thousand years before the birth of Christ, in the cold, damp lands of central Europe, people of the Celtic race developed one of the most eerily fascinating faiths ever practiced. One aspect of the distinctive religion is now referred to as the Cult of the Head.

The Celts revered the human head as Christians do the cross. To them, the head housed the soul and thus reflected divinity, so they surrounded themselves with heads, real and crafted.

Enemies taken in battle furnished an ample supply of the grisly trophies, and joyous celebration accompanied each new acquisition. Upon decapitat-ing a respected foe, a warrior would sing a hymn of praise as he charged home triumphantly. Ritual sacrifice of human beings also provided heads, which the Celtic priests known as Druids offered up to the gods.

The Celts decorated temples with the skulls and proudly exhibited them in their homes, often drinking wine from vessels wrought out of the craniums. They also fashioned artificial heads from wood, stone, and metal. These icons adorned houses, clothing, weap-onry, and horses' tack, supposedly bestowing good luck, warding off evil, and even healing wounds.

Sacred skulls flank a reconstructed doorway (left) from a Celtic shrine in southeastern France. So compelling was the Cult of the Head that it persisted even after the Celtic civilization began to wane in the first century BC: The bronze head below, found at Glastonbury Tor, was made about AD 600. Pictish warriors like the one depicted at right were also obsessed with the head; such fighters may have battled with Arthur in Britain.

Saucers. According to an old Cornish folk belief, Arthur turned into a bird—a raven in some versions of the story, a red-legged chough in others—and still lives above the raging sea on Tintagel's lofty cliffs. Another folk belief is that on certain nights the original Round Table can be seen rising out of the mist of a local pond. In fact, legends regarding Arthur, Merlin, and the rest of their romantic crew have sprouted up in nearly every nook and cranny of Tintagel Castle and its environs.

Arthur's larger-than-life reputation as a great military leader can be found in the folklore and superstitions of the towns and villages where he reportedly waged his battles. At Cefn Bryn in Wales, for example, local legend suggests that a large, flat stone on the village commons is a pebble that Arthur found in his shoe while marching to his fate at the battle of Camlan. The great king supposedly removed the stone, then flung it seven miles to its present location. For many years, young women from the village would use the stone to test their sweethearts' fidelity. At midnight under a full moon, a girl would place a freshly baked barley cake on top of the slab of rock and then crawl around it three times on her hands and knees. If her lover appeared in the moonlight at the end of this ritual, the woman would know he was faithful to her; if he did not turn up, then she would know his troth was false.

The search for Camelot, the home and headquarters for Arthur and his brotherhood of knights, has centered on Cadbury Hill, an Iron Age fort on a 500-foot-high plateau near the Somerset village of South Cadbury. This hill was never home to a castle in the medieval sense, but its ancient earthworks made it a formidable citadel, and it was used many times as a defensive stronghold in centuries past. No one knows the names of the leaders or kings who lived there. Flowing nearby is a small river on whose shores Arthur may have fought his last battle. An alternative theory supposes that the battle of Camlan was fought near Camelford in Cornwall.

The association of Cadbury Hill with Camelot can be traced back to John Leland, a sixteenth-century antiquary who spent much of his life researching Arthurian legends. In 1542, after a trip to South Cadbury, Leland wrote: "At the very south end of the church of South-Cadbyri standeth Camallate, sometime a famous town or castle. . . . The people can tell nothing there but that they have heard say Arthur much resorted to Camalat." In later centuries, the villagers of South Cadbury called the highest part of the hill Arthur's Palace and told a haunting tale about a pair of gates, hidden in the hillside, that swung open once a year to reveal King Arthur and his court, fast asleep.

Another local legend recorded by folklorists recounted how Arthur and his knights, every year on Midsummer Eve and Christmas Eve, rode down from the hill to drink from a spring beside the village church. The villagers hearkened to the clatter of the horses' hoofs, which they believed to be shod with silver.

For four years during the late 1960s, archaeologists dug in selected areas of Cadbury Hill, searching for evidence that would link this isolated spot to the fabled King Arthur. Calling their project the Quest for Camelot, the archaeologists found that Cadbury Hill's four great man-made ridges had been rebuilt time and again over a period of 5,000 years. During the first century, the fortress was stormed and captured by the Romans, only to be subsequently abandoned. Several hundred years later, around the time of Arthur, the new inhabitants of this region erected a number of buildings on the uppermost portion of the hill (Arthur's Palace), including a Roman-style gatehouse and a great timbered hall.

The most striking and sophisticated structure, however, was a circular stone-and-timber wall measuring about sixteen feet thick and nearly three-quarters of a mile long. Both the design and workmanship of the wall were Celtic, not Roman, suggesting that whoever ordered it built was an admirer of traditional Celtic ways. And as no other structure of its size and kind has been uncovered in Britain, archaeologists believe the ruler who oversaw its construction must have had unparalleled resources of men and money at his disposal. Such a description, of course, fits King Arthur.

"The conclusion is inescapable that [Cadbury Hill] was the fortress of a great military leader, a man in a unique position, with special responsibilities and an unusual temper of mind," wrote Leslie Alcock and Geoffrey Ashe, two of the archaeologists and historians involved with the Quest for Camelot excavation. Nothing was unearthed at the site to prove that the leader who lived there was named Arthur, but Alcock and Ashe insisted that the question of the name is "hardly more than a quibble." The man who ruled Cadbury Hill during its spectacular sixth-century refortification, they noted, was as much like Arthur as anyone could be at the time, certainly "a person big enough for the legends to have gathered round him."

Only eleven miles away is Glastonbury, a sacred site steeped in magic and legend, dating back to pagan times. Tradition holds that this place was once the otherworldly Isle of Avalon, where Arthur was brought to have his wounds healed by Morgan le Fay. Today, Glastonbury is a busy market town set among flat, low-lying meadows. But centuries ago the community was set apart on an inland island, surrounded by marshes that have since been drained. Its ancient Celtic name was Ynis Witrin, or Glass Island.

According to legend, Christianity came early to Glastonbury. Joseph of Arimathea, who had taken the body of Jesus and placed it in his own tomb, is said to have settled in the village during the first century, bringing with him twelve missionaries and the Holy Grail—the chalice from which Christ drank at the Last Supper. A small wattle-and-daub church, which stood on the grounds of Glastonbury Abbey until the twelfth century, was reportedly built by Joseph and his followers.

During the Middle Ages, the church, with its collection of sacred relics and its reputation as the first Christian church in Britain, became a popular place of pilgrimage. Many people came to see the remains of Saint Patrick, the patron saint of Ireland, who was said to have died in Glastonbury at the age of 111 after establishing a monastery there during the fifth century. Despite the legends of Joseph

Homage to the Mother Goddess

A number of mystical sites in Britain share a particularly rich and varied history, having figured in Druid and Christian worship, in Arthurian legend, and in New Age spirituality. But even the earliest of these associations is relatively new compared with the beginnings of the sacred landmarks. Six thousand years ago, or more, some of the sites were holy ground for an earlier, earthier people—the Neolithic worshipers of the Mother Goddess.

The goddess, an earth-mother deity revered by primitive societies in many parts of the world, apparently had a following in England. Silbury Hill *(below)*, a huge earthen mound near Stonehenge, is believed by some to have represented the goddess's belly, heavy with child. Its creation required a prodigious effort that may have lasted fifteen years; the builders had to lug about 36 million baskets of earth.

One mile east of the town of Glastonbury stands another colossal earth pregnancy, the 500-foot-high Tor *(far right)*. Terraces etched in the sides of this natural hill form a labyrinth that some say figured in the goddess cult's rituals of initiation. According to that scenario, novices were sent to wander lost through the maze, eventually to discover their way in a symbolic passage of death and rebirth.

The mysterious egg-shaped boulder at right was discovered early in this century and lent credence to the notion of a flowering of the goddess cult. Some scholars believe the three-foot-long stone was a talisman to fertility.

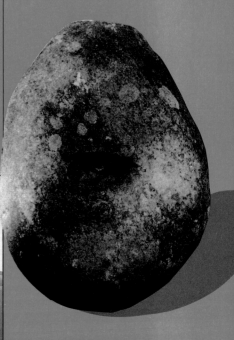

Thought to be a symbol for the powerful Cosmic Mother, the egg-stone (below) may possess a force of its own: Dowsers claim it emits strong vibrations of energy.

At 130 feet, Silbury Hill (left) is the tallest artificial structure still remaining from the prehistoric era in Europe; it is also one of the most mysterious. Some historians believe that it represents an eye, one of the familiar symbols of the Mother Goddess: The hill itself forms her iris, and the circle at the top, her pupil.

Rising majestically from the flatlands that surround it and capped with the ruins of a church dedicated to Saint Michael, Glastonbury Tor is an unmistakable landmark from the air. This visual prominence has led some people to indulge in speculation about the Tor's use as a flying-saucer landing pad.

of Arimathea, however, the Holy Grail was not found among the sacred items enshrined at the old church.

Glastonbury is dominated by the Tor, an extraordinary, 500-foot-high cone visible from all directions for up to twenty miles. Motorists catching sight of Glastonbury Tor for the first time will often pull over to the side of the road and gaze for a while in wonder. The word *hill* is inadequate; the Tor is more like a conical pile of earth rising from the plain on which it rests. Around its sides are man-made terraces that form a huge labyrinth winding to the top. Some scholars believe these tortuous paths were designed for use in prehistoric pagan rituals.

The Tor is crowned with the ruined tower of a church dedicated to Saint Michael, a celebrated slayer of dragons and destroyer of evil spirits. Medieval monks built the church to Christianize the site and take away its association with pagan kings and gods. According to one ancient Celtic legend, the entrance to Annwn, the underworld home of the fairies, can be found within the natural water tunnels and chambers beneath the Tor. It is from this portal that Gwynn ap Nudd, king of the fairies, is said to set out on wild hunts to find and steal the spirits of the dead.

A number of local legends suggest a connection between Arthur and Glastonbury Tor. In one, Arthur travels to Annwn to steal the magic cauldron of plenty from the fairies. In another, he rescues Guinevere from the hill, where she has been imprisoned by King Melwas of Somerset. This story may be based on historical fact, for archaeologists recently discovered evidence that a medieval citadel once stood on the Tor, pointing to the presence of a king based there during Arthur's era.

Although one tradition has it that Arthur still lives, sleeping on the Isle of Avalon, another story describes how he died from wounds incurred at the battle of Camlan and was buried at some unknown location. In an old Welsh poem called *The Song of the Graves,* Arthur is the only famous warrior whose place of burial is not named. "A mystery to the world, the grave of Arthur," wrote the poet, and a mystery it remains to this day.

The secret was thought to have been uncovered in the latter half of the twelfth century, when King Henry II reported that a wandering Welsh bard had told him Arthur was buried in Glastonbury Abbey's graveyard. According to this source, the tomb was between two "pyramids," or memorial pillars. Henry passed this information to the abbot of Glastonbury, but no attempt was made to locate the grave until after a fire had destroyed much of the abbey, including the old wattle church, in 1184.

During the rebuilding of the abbey, the abbot ordered a search for Arthur's grave, and excavations were carried out. At a depth of seven feet, the diggers uncovered a stone slab and, beneath that, a lead cross bearing the inscription *Hic iacet sepultus inclitus rex arturius in insula avalonia,* or "Here lies buried the renowned King Arthur in the Isle of Avalon." Another nine feet down, they came upon the coffin, which had been fashioned from a hollowed-out log. Inside were the bones of a tall man whose skull had been fractured grotesquely. The abbot's team interpreted this injury as a sign that the man had been killed by a blow to the head. Some smaller bones and a lock of yellow hair were also discovered in the coffin, although the latter reportedly disintegrated when it was touched. The monks believed that these other remains were those of Guinevere.

The bones were placed in two elaborately carved tombs and set in the abbey, where they stayed enshrined for almost a century. In 1278, in the presence of King Edward I, they were unearthed once again. "The lord Edward . . . with his consort, the lady Eleanor, came to Glastonbury . . . to celebrate Easter," wrote one Adam of Domerham, who observed the event. "The following Tuesday . . . at dusk, the lord king had the tomb of the famous King Arthur opened. Wherein, in two caskets painted with their pictures and arms, were found separatedly the bones of the said king, which were of great size, and those of Queen Guinevere, which were of marvellous beauty. On the following day . . . the lord king replaced the bones of the king and the queen, each in their own casket, having wrapped them in

The legend of Arthur had woven itself tightly into the fabric of British culture by the fifteenth century, when this stone sculpture of the heroic king was carved. The memory—or fantasy—of his grand existence fueled much of the nation's literature, philosophy, even politics, for centuries.

The frigid waters of the Celtic Sea pound the shore at Arthur's Head (below), a craggy promontory beneath Tintagel Castle, the supposed birthplace of the fabled king. The sorcerer Merlin is said to haunt the dank cave nearby (left). And, indeed, as the tide rises and the salt sea foams through the jagged opening, one can hear eerie noises from deep within the cave that sound like a man moaning or sighing.

costly silks. When they had been sealed they ordered the tomb to be placed forthwith in front of the high altar, after the removal of the skulls for the veneration of the people."

There the bones lay until 1539, when King Henry VIII's agents seized the abbey, murdered its abbot, stole the treasures, and left the church to fall into ruin. One of the items lost in the looting was the cross that had marked Arthur's grave. The remains of Arthur and Guinevere were dispersed to other locations and eventually disappeared.

Some historians think the uncovering of Arthur's grave at Glastonbury Abbey may actually have been a hoax. It was, they say, instigated by the monks, who wanted to raise money to rebuild their monastery—a scheme abetted indirectly by Henry II. These doubters speculate that King Henry's real aim may have been to weaken Welsh resistance to British rule by proving that Arthur was dead and thus unable to come back and champion the Celtic cause. In 1962, however, excavations conducted at Glastonbury Abbey by British archaeologist Ralegh Radford revealed that twelfth-century monks had, indeed, dug on the abbey grounds between two ancient "pyramids," or crosses, and that they had uncovered a very deep grave. Radford conscientiously noted that the excavations did not reveal to whom the grave belonged.

One of the most notorious excavations at Glastonbury Abbey occurred earlier in the twentieth century, soon after the Church of England bought the desolate shell of the abbey in 1907. By then, the once mighty edifice was ruined beyond any possibility of restoration; most of the stones from the fallen structure had been sold for use in the construction of buildings in and around Glastonbury. No one could tell any longer where the monks had lived, so to better understand the abbey's history, the Church decided to excavate the site.

The man chosen to direct the project was Frederick Bligh Bond, a moody and eccentric architect who was an expert on Gothic architecture and specialized in the study of old churches. Although he had very few historical records to guide him, Bond was uncannily successful from the start,

Crumbling arches and buttresses stand their ground amid the ruins of Glastonbury Abbey, where Frederick Bligh Bond directed excavations of the fallen monastery. Bond believed he had established the location of the lost Loretto Chapel, mentioned in the scribbled Latin notes below. The alleged source of the messages was a long-dead monk with whom Bond communicated by means of automatic writing.

uncovering the foundations of five chapels; the monks' dormitory, kitchen, and refectory; a glass-and-pottery kiln; and several other previously unknown rooms and structures.

Bond's accuracy in choosing the right places to dig was phenomenal. One of his main assigned tasks was to find the lost Edgar Chapel, which had been built just before the abbey was destroyed by Henry VIII's vandals. Bond insisted on looking for the chapel on the east end of the abbey, a site other experts thought unlikely for such an important sanctuary. He even predicted the length of the chapel—592 feet. Incredibly, the excavators found the chapel exactly where their leader had said it would be—and it was precisely 592 feet long.

For almost a decade, Bond publicly attributed his successes at Glastonbury Abbey to instinct and good luck. Then, in 1918 he published a book entitled *The Gate of Remembrance,* in which he revealed what he called the true story behind his excavations. His successes, he said, had been made possible by communications with the spirits of more than two dozen long-dead residents of Glastonbury, including monks, knights, a clockmaker, a master mason, and a cowherd.

For the communications, Bond had relied on a spiritualist friend, John Alleyne Bartlett, who claimed to be a medium for the written messages of departed spirits through an occult practice known as automatic writing. Bartlett alleged that his hand would glide across the page without any mental input on his part, the pencil directed by an intelligence not his own. With Bond asking the questions and Bartlett writing down the often enigmatic answers, page after page of comments, diagrams, and historical anecdotes were gathered from the Company of Avalon, as the group of spirits purportedly called themselves.

Bond said it was one of the abbey's long-dead clerics, Gulielmus Monachus, or William the Monk, who had first led him to the site of Edgar Chapel. William had—supposedly—also explained the contents of a mysterious grave on the south side of the abbey nave; in it, a skeleton had been discovered with the skull of another man nestled between

its knees. According to William, the remains were those of Radulphus Cancellarius, or Radulphus the Treasurer. "He, dying, after many years desired that they who loved him should bury him without the church where he was wont to feed the birds in his chair," William's spirit told Bond. "The sun did shine there as he loved it for his blood was cold." Unknown to Radulphus's mourners, William added, the skeleton of a man whom Radulphus had killed many years earlier had been buried in exactly that spot. Thus, the bones of two mortal enemies had come to rest in a single grave.

Not all of the stories passed along by the abbey spirits were so macabre. In addition to providing details about the Glastonbury buildings, some of the communications from beyond the grave were taken up with intimate secrets. Perhaps the most engaging character in the Company of Avalon was a monk by the name of Johannes, who had a touching concern about his stoutness: "Soe I remember those stayres for my fatness, but it availed me not. Tho' my Father Prior recommended it off. Alas, I waxed more fat. Not that my belly was my god, I wot not! But I was cheery and troubled not. . . . So said I, 'It is the Lord's will. Somme he made fat and somme be lean' and this I said to they that jibed, that the Gates of Heaven are made full wide for all sorts, so that none created should stick within the portall. This I said, for they vexed me with their quips."

In another of his revelations, Johannes opened his heart about a rather innocent brush with romance that befell him one day when he was ferrying a young woman across a river: "I have a sin—of all innocence I must confess," he said. "The Hussey kissed my hot cheek before I could say 'Stop' or say a prayer to St. Anthony. It's true I rubbed it off with the tail of my habit—but the memory remained and there is an unholy gladness that I could not rid myself of. I did penance by mopping the Refectory floor on bended knees, yet glad was I for the kiss and am to this day. Lord have mercy on mine o'er tainted soul."

The publication of Bond's book caused something of

A drawing of an enthroned Prester John flags the location of his mysterious land—in what is now Ethiopia—on this 1558 Portuguese map. The supposed priest-king's letter 400 years earlier had boasted of a realm encompassing India and part of Africa.

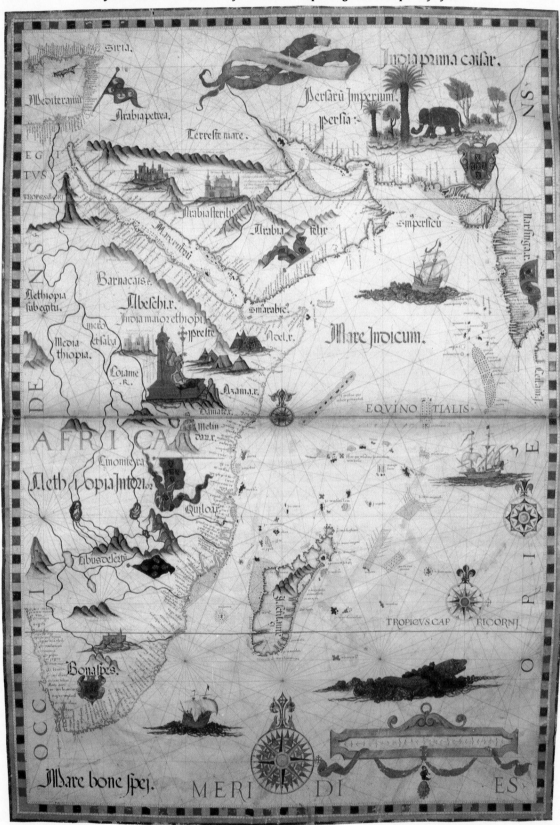

*Fourteenth-century author Sir John Mandeville wrote a
fanciful travelogue in which he claimed to have visited Prester John's kingdom. He
accompanied his narrative with drawings like those below.*

*Mandeville wrote that the desert
men of Prester John's land "be horned,
and they grunt, as pigs."*

*"Under a rock," he continued,
"is an head and the visage of a devil, full
horrible and dreadful to see."*

*There was also a beast with
"three long horns, sharp as a sword," that
"chaseth and slayeth the elephant."*

an uproar. Church authorities were outraged that the architect had connected spiritualism with the excavation of the abbey, and they quickly appointed a new supervisor for the project. By 1921, Bond was reduced to cataloging and cleaning artifacts from his earlier discoveries. A year later, he was fired and banned from the abbey grounds, his career, like the abbey itself, in ruins. The Church ordered an end to the excavation, and some of the foundation walls Bond had unearthed were removed or covered with turf. Bond lived another twenty-three years, writing several other books about the Company of Avalon and other psychic phenomena. He died in 1945, poor and embittered.

The attributes of Camelot—a kingdom of peace and abundance ruled by a just and courageous king—were also attached to another mysterious monarchy of the Middle Ages, that of the legendary Prester John. *Prester* is a shortened form of *presbyter,* a title sometimes used for priests and elders. The proper name may have come from John, the apostle who wrote the Fourth Gospel. If Prester John's empire was as magnificent as some accounts maintained, the glories of Rome and Constantinople were trivial by comparison. The imagination soars at the possibilities of what he might have done for Christendom if he had ever marched his legions into Europe.

The story of the warrior-king Prester John apparently first reached Europe in 1145 with the arrival in Rome of a Syrian prelate, Bishop Hugh of Jabala. The bishop's homeland had been seized by Muslims, and he had traveled to Rome to appeal for aid from Pope Eugenius III. While in Rome, Bishop Hugh told a wondrous tale of a powerful Christian monarch named John, who ruled the lands beyond Persia. This king, said the bishop, belonged to an eastern branch of Christianity known as the Nestorian Church, and he had recently led his followers in a decisive victory against the Muslims. Church authorities in Rome were pleased to hear such news, for it was the time of the Crusades, when Christians were trying to recover the Holy Land from the warriors of Islam.

Some historians believe Bishop Hugh may have been referring to the Turkish army's defeat in 1141 at the battle of Qatwan in Persia. If so, the bishop had a central element of his story wrong, for it was not a Christian conqueror but a Mongol warlord known as Gur Khan who overpowered the Turks. Many Nestorians were among Gur Khan's followers, and they may have Latinized his name as Johannes, or John.

The idea of a faraway Christian empire ruled by a fearless priest-king quickly took hold among Europeans of the Dark Ages. Prester John's reputation grew steadily, so that before too long he possessed royal lineage and enormous wealth. A twelfth-century historian who had interviewed Bishop Hugh wrote: "It is said that he is a lineal descendant of the Magi, of whom mention is made in the Gospel. And that ruling over the same peoples which they governed he enjoys such great glory and wealth that he uses no scepter save one of emerald."

Prester John's fame took wing in 1165, when Manuel I Comnenus, emperor of the Eastern Roman Empire, received an extraordinary letter (written in Latin) from a man who signed himself "Presbyter Johannes, by the power and virtue of God and of the Lord Jesus Christ, Lord of Lords." The letter writer said he surpassed "all the kings of the whole earth in riches, mercy and omnipotence," and that no fewer than seventy-two other kings paid him tribute. His empire, he boasted, was free of evil and vice. And he declared: "Our land streams with honey, and is overflowing with milk. In one region grows no poisonous herb, nor does a querulous frog ever quack in it, no scorpion exists, nor does the serpent glide amongst the grass, nor can any poisonous animals exist in it or injure any one. With us no one lies, for he who speaks a lie is thenceforth regarded as dead."

Manuel forwarded the letter to Frederick Barbarossa, Holy Roman emperor and king of Germany. A dozen years after its first appearance, Pope Alexander III reportedly answered it, demanding that Prester John recognize the pope's ultimate authority over his lands. Just who, if anyone, received the pope's response is unknown, for the messenger who carried the letter eastward never returned. Prester John's self-extolling letter, however, was translated into several languages and circulated throughout Europe. Embellishments accompanied each new translation, and it became very popular reading. Prester John was said to live in a crystal palace and to sleep on a bed of sapphires. His robes were sewn from salamander wool and cleaned in fire. He rode flying dragons and owned a magic mirror in which he could see everything going on in his kingdom and thwart any conspiracy that might be brewing against him.

One passage in the letter revealed a key factor in Prester John's military successes. Under his rule, it stated, was a race that routinely ate human flesh and knew no fear of death. "When any of these people die," wrote Prester John (or whoever used his name), "their friends and relations eat him ravenously, for they regard it as a main duty to munch human flesh. We lead them at our pleasure against our foes, and neither man nor beast is left undevoured.

The hill fortress of Great Zimbabwe dwarfs the Great Enclosure, depicted in the middle ground in German geologist Karl Mauch's 1871 sketch (left). While the purpose of the hill fortress is clear—it provided defense—that of the Great Enclosure (below) has inspired debate ever since Mauch's first visit. Unlike virtually any other ancient stone ruin, it follows no regular geometric plan, being elliptical rather than circular, like Stonehenge, or rectangular, like the Pyramids. One scholar believes the strange internal passage shown in the photograph at right funneled captives in and out of the complex, which may have served as a slave market.

When all our foes are eaten, then we return with our hosts home again." In a German version of the letter, parts of Prester John's kingdom were occupied by many other strange creatures, including "wild people who have horns on their heads" and who "yelp and grunt like pigs"; mice and ants who dig for gold and other precious metals; and the *sidicus,* a beautiful green and red bird who has "a tongue like that of a man" and can converse with humans.

In 1221, an exciting new rumor reached Rome. A Christian king was crushing Muslim armies in the East. The king's name was reported to be David, the grandson of Prester John. Historians have said there was some truth to the rumor, although the king was not Christian and his name was not David but Genghis Khan. The bloodthirsty horsemen of the Mongol conqueror swept across Asia early in the thirteenth century, overwhelming everything in their path.

For many years afterward, various adventurers, including Marco Polo, searched for Prester John's kingdom, but without success. When Polo returned to Venice in 1295, he reported on the wonders and riches in the court of Kublai Khan, grandson of the conqueror Genghis Khan, but said that he had not discovered any evidence of Prester John's empire. So strong was the Prester John legend, however, that many people thought Polo must have been lying. The great explorer did tell of Ung Khan, a Christian ruler whose central Asian kingdom had been demolished years earlier by Genghis Khan. But Ung Khan would have been too young to be Prester John, and there was nothing magical or even special about his kingdom. People could not believe that such an ordinary king could have any connection with the fabled monarch.

Eventually, as central Asia was explored by Europe-

The Great Enclosure's massive conical tower may reveal that the site was a temple of phallic worship, like the one on this Phoenician coin.

ans, who found no evidence of Prester John's kingdom, storytellers transported the legend to Africa. During the fifteenth century, Prince Henry the Navigator of Portugal instructed his captains to search for the priest-king's lost land during their voyages around Africa. When Vasco da Gama landed his ships at Mozambique in 1497, he dutifully jotted in his logbook the rumors he heard about the Christian king: "We were told that Prester John resided not far from this place; that he held many cities along the coast and the inhabitants of these cities were great merchants and owned big ships."

The African country associated most clearly with the story of Prester John is Abyssinia, now Ethiopia, a region of Africa that was Christian from the fourth century. In fact, the first European book written about Ethiopia, published in 1540, referred to that country's king as Prester John, or "the Preste." Some scholars have suggested that the ancient Abyssinian royal title *zan* was incorrectly rendered as "John" and that this confusion is the true source of the Prester John legend.

Adding weight to this argument is the discovery of ancient Christian banners and swords by Portuguese missionaries serving in Ethiopia early in the twentieth century. The families that had tended the banners and swords for generations reported that they had once belonged to an all-powerful Christian king. So convinced were Europeans of the authenticity of the tale that they continued for decades to place Prester John's name on maps of Africa—just where the word *Ethiopia* is found today.

Just as explorers searched for centuries for Prester John's kingdom, so they ranged far and wide hoping to find the biblical land of Ophir, from which King Solomon was said to have obtained his treasures of gold, precious gems, and ivory. By the sixteenth century, many of those who sought this lost land believed that it must be located in southern Africa. Arab traders living along the East African coast told adventurers from Europe tantalizing stories of a great inland kingdom with immense stone fortresses guarding ancient gold mines.

In 1551, Portuguese historian João de Barros published a book, *Décadas da Asia,* in which he related what Arab traders had told him about the largest of these stone fortresses: "[It] is a square fortress of masonry within and without, built of stones of marvellous size, and there appears to be no mortar joining them." Above the door of the fortress was an inscription that neither the Arabs nor the Africans could decipher, and this convinced Barros that the building was of non-African origin.

The idea that this ancient fortress was linked to the biblical Ophir did not really take hold, however, until 1872. That was the year a young, self-educated German geologist named Karl Gottlieb Mauch returned home to publish the story of his harrowing journey into the African interior in search of the fabled stone fortress. Mauch had first arrived in southern Africa in 1865, when he was twenty-eight years old. He wanted to make a name for himself as a great scientist-explorer, but he could not afford an elaborate expedition. He thus roamed alone through the bush, wearing a many-pocketed leather outfit of his own design and carrying sixty pounds of astronomical and meteorological instruments and books. Among his other trappings were an umbrella to shade him from the sun, a woolen blanket for cold nights, a long knife, and two guns, one of which, he said, was "able to kill an elephant as well as a rabbit." According to his own descriptions, he looked like an itinerant Robinson Crusoe.

Mauch wandered around the southern tip of Africa for several years, testing soil samples, analyzing rocks, and making many maps, including the first complete map of Transvaal. He also discovered several rich gold fields, but he did not attempt to mine them, being more interested in his scientific endeavors. Then, in 1867, Mauch heard descriptions of mysterious stone ruins lying many miles west of the coastal city of Sofala, Mozambique. The ruins were said to have once been the capital of a vast empire ruled by a powerful king.

Intrigued by the stories of a lost city and believing that it might be Ophir, Mauch soon determined to locate and examine the ruins. He wrote in his journal: "I shall make it the highest duty in my profession to add honour to the name of the German nation. . . . The discovery of the ruins of Ophir would be a point which would have to be envied by other nations."

On July 3, 1871, Mauch set out with a few African porters for a little-known region west of Mozambique, between the Limpopo and Zambezi rivers—an area that he considered to be the most likely location of the ruins. The journey was difficult and dangerous. Food and water were often scarce; at one point, Mauch and his porters, weak with hunger, chewed their buffalo-hide sandals for nourishment. Then he was captured and imprisoned by a local chieftain. Fortunately, an old German-American ivory hunter named Adam Renders lived nearby and came to Mauch's rescue, prompting the chief to let the explorer go free in exchange for a small gift.

Nearly broken in spirit and health, Mauch considered returning to Europe, but Renders persuaded him not to abandon his quest. The ruins that Mauch had come so far to see, explained Renders, were not far away. In fact, added the veteran hunter, he had camped there himself several times during the past few years. Renders agreed to lead Mauch to the site of the ruins.

On September 5, 1871, Karl Mauch climbed a hill known as Ghost Mountain and beheld, half-hidden amid brush and acacia trees about eight miles away, the crumbling fortress he had endured so much to visit. He later wrote of his excitement and relief upon seeing the ruins for the first time: " 'Bravo' I exclaimed, 'that is what I have been seeking since 1868. What luck! And how unexpected!—Only a few days before, occupied with serious thoughts of death, and to-day standing before the most brilliant success of my travels. God be praised!' "

What Mauch saw in the valley before him were two colossal ruins, which still dominate the site today and are known as Great Zimbabwe. One of the structures, the hill fortress, sits among huge, strangely shaped granite boulders and outcrops. Standing on a lower hill about a quarter of a mile away is a large elliptical building called the Great Enclosure. The outer wall, 830 feet around and up to 35 feet high, is made of large blocks of granite laid without mortar. Within the outer wall are many inner walls that form rooms and narrow passages.

The Great Enclosure also contains an imposing thirty-four-foot-high structure known as the conical tower. With no opening of any kind and no stairs, the tower remains a great mystery to archaeologists. Some of them believe it was a phallic symbol; others claim it must have been used as an astronomical observatory; and still others suspect that it was nothing more than a fire tower or a sentry post. Another, smaller, tower once stood nearby, but it has long since crumbled.

Great Zimbabwe is just one of about 8,000 stone ruins that have been found in southern Africa. But it is by far the most spectacular, perhaps the greatest stone structure on the African continent outside Egypt. It is from these ruins that the country of Zimbabwe—formerly Rhodesia—took its name when its black majority assumed control in 1979 from the earlier colonial government.

Just who built Great Zimbabwe, and why, is still unknown. Karl Mauch believed that the ruins were the remains of the kingdom of Ophir. The hill fortress, he suggested, was built as a replica of King Solomon's temple on Mount Moriah in Palestine, and the Great Enclosure was a copy of a palace where the opulent Queen of Sheba had visited Solomon before their marriage. Mauch even proposed that the queen had been involved in the planning and construction of the Great Zimbabwe structures, importing Phoenician masons to carry out the work.

Most modern archaeologists and anthropologists, however, believe that Great Zimbabwe was built and occupied by Africans, not by people from distant lands. The city was most likely founded during the ninth century as the major trading center of a great Bantu-speaking mining nation, and it remained vibrant until the fifteenth century. At its peak, Great Zimbabwe may have been home to as many as 10,000 people. Potsherds and beads from Arabia, India, and China have been excavated at the site, indicating that the gold and other precious metals extracted from nearby mines drew traders from distant ports.

Great Zimbabwe, or Zimbabye, was not only a commercial hub but a great religious center. Eight large soapstone birds, powerful icons of a forgotten people, were found at the site—seven in the hill fortress and one in the stony rubble between the fortress and the Great Enclosure. On the most elaborately carved of these soapstones, a crocodile is depicted crawling upward toward a strong, sleek bird perched on top. The bird is now the national emblem of modern Zimbabwe.

When Mauch returned to Europe, his writings about the ruins of Great Zimbabwe caught the fancy and fascination of the public. Many adventurers—some looking for gold, others for archaeological evidence of King Solomon's rule—set off for southern Africa. Unfortunately, these plunderers and amateur excavators destroyed much of what remained at Great Zimbabwe before it became clear that the nearby mines had been emptied of their gold years before, and that the ruined buildings were not old enough to have belonged to Solomon. Nevertheless, the legend endured. Novelist Sir Henry Rider Haggard made it even larger when he used Great Zimbabwe as one of the major settings in his work *King Solomon's Mines*.

Mauch himself never returned to Great Zimbabwe. In 1874, apparently delirious from a recurrence of malaria, he either fell or jumped from the window of his house in Würtemberg, Germany, and he died soon afterward. He was only thirty-seven years old. On Mauch's gravestone are etched the commemorative words: "Discoverer of the Ruins of Zimbabye."

Where History Falls Silent

For nearly as long as humans have felt the urge to settle in fixed communities, they have signified their intention by building temples and towns of stone. Many of these efforts proved to be false starts and left behind mystifying traces of vanished ways of life. A few fascinating archaic cultures disappeared almost without a trace. They left no great works of literature, no lasting contributions to government, philosophy, or science. In some cases, even their names were lost—their legacies reduced to the timeworn stones they once set in place.

These enigmatic ruins offer little but the mute insistence of their presence. The following pages examine an assortment of abandoned cities and shrines, all of which have guarded their secrets well. From the rose-colored necropolis of Petra, in Jordan, to New Mexico's ancient adobe apartment buildings, they tantalize with unanswered riddles. Cambodia's Angkor Wat, the exquisite temple-tomb of a Khmer god-king, was once thought explainable only as "the work of giants." The written language of Pakistan's prehistoric Mohenjo-Daro still awaits deciphering.

For the inhabitants of a few of these settlements, archaeologists and historians have pieced together a fairly vivid picture of everyday life. But the new understanding merely brings additional questions: What inspired such vast building projects? And what led the builders to abandon their extraordinary creations? Science and careful study have ferreted out a few explanations but can only leave it to the imagination to grapple with the puzzles that remain.

Angkor Wat is one of hundreds of ruined temples in Angkor, once a sprawling center of religious devotion in the jungles of Cambodia. Angkor was the capital of the Khmer empire, which ruled Southeast Asia for 600 years into the fifteenth century. The Khmer god-kings, worshiped as embodiments of the Hindu gods Vishnu and Shiva, commissioned the building of magnificent temples, which eventually served as their tombs. None of the other monuments equaled Angkor Wat, with its graceful terraces, lotus-bud towers, and miles of intricate bas-relief ornamentation. To Henri Mouhot, the French naturalist who discovered the ruins in 1860, the temple was "grander than anything left to us by Greece or Rome." The complex was conceived as a model of the Hindu cosmos, with five towers representing Mount Meru—believed to be the center of the universe—and a wide moat symbolizing the seven cosmic seas. But just as religious fervor had brought the temples into being, a change of faith is thought to have sped their decline. As the people turned from Hinduism to the quiet ways of Buddhism, the worship of godly kings became a thing of the past. And, as the Khmer empire collapsed, the tombs of its rulers were left to the mercy of the jungle.

Machu Picchu, a fifteenth-century Inca citadel in the Peruvian Andes, reveals the consummate craftsmanship of its builders but little about their fate. The temples, palaces, fountains, and terraces of the city were constructed of white-granite stones so expertly fitted that they required no mortar in the joints. West of the ruins is a carved stone outcrop (above) known as Intihuatana, or "hitching post of the sun." Here, ancient priests symbolically tethered the sun god Inti during the winter solstice, hoping to ensure his return in the summer. Machu Picchu may also have included a convent for Inti's female devotees, who were known as Virgins of the Sun.

The lost city came to the attention of scholars in North America and Europe in 1911, when a local farmer showed it to Hiram Bingham, a visiting Yale historian. Bingham assumed he had stumbled upon Vilcabamba, the legendary final outpost of Inca civilization. That theory was disproved, however, and researchers have never determined what drove away Machu Picchu's inhabitants. The explanation may lie in an epidemic or war—or in a particularly gruesome Inca custom: According to tradition, all of a man's kin were ritually executed, along with his neighbors and livestock, if he committed the unpardonable sin of defiling a Virgin of the Sun.

Hewn from sandstone cliffs in a mountainous region of southwestern Jordan more than 2,000 years ago, Petra prospered for seven centuries at the crossroads of two great caravan routes. Its builders were the Nabataeans, a desert tribe whose principal deity, Dusares, was represented by a rugged block of stone. Their architectural masterpiece was the Khazneh, or "treasury," shown at left and above. This monument was probably the tomb of some great, forgotten king, but it was named for a fabled cache of treasure that a pharaoh supposedly stored in the urn that adorns its pinnacle. In the photograph above, the facade of the Khazneh greets visitors at the end of a narrow, mile-and-a-half-long gorge, which was the only way in or out of Petra. Swallowed, in turn, by the Roman and Byzantine empires, battered by a terrible fourth-century earthquake, then abandoned for good when the trade routes shifted to bypass this part of the desert, the silent stone city was rediscovered in 1812 by a Swiss explorer named Johann Ludwig Burckhardt.

According to legend, the Tellem tribesmen who once scaled the Bandiagara cliffs of Mali (above) did so with the aid of magic. They could fly or—in a pinch—could extend their bodies so as to climb in a single step to the highest caves. More likely, the Tellem, who vanished in the sixteenth century, used ropes. In the high caves they stored their grain and interred their dead; on the ground they left few traces of their way of life. The land is now home to a people called the Dogon, whose thatched granaries and flat-roofed homes (right) are built in the scree at the foot of the cliffs. Though unrelated to the Tellem, the Dogon revere the earlier residents. They also present enigmas of their own: Despite a subsistence-farming lifestyle and a lack of telescopes, they know of several celestial features, such as the moons of Jupiter, that are invisible to the naked eye.

When it was built forty-five centuries ago, Mohenjo-Daro was in many ways a city of the future. A center of the lost Indus Valley civilization in what is now Pakistan, it was meticulously laid out with twelve broad avenues intersecting narrower streets to form a grid of city blocks (above). Buildings were made of brick, and a network of earthenware pipes and gutters carried wastewater from bathrooms, some of which were equipped with toilets. The city, home to 40,000, was a thriving hub of agriculture, manufacturing, and commerce. Public life centered around the citadel, which contained meeting halls, offices, a granary, and baths.

It is not at all clear why Mohenjo-Daro was abandoned after a thousand years. Archaeologists believe that the city was increasingly plagued by floods, brought on perhaps by excessive woodcutting needed to fuel the brickmaking kilns. Battered skeletal remains also seem to indicate an incursion by armed invaders. The city lay buried until 1922 under the mound that provided its name—Mohenjo-Daro translates as ''hill of the dead.'' An ancient curse associated with the site may have protected it from vandals till then: Legend held that anyone foolish enough to climb the hill ran the risk of turning bright blue.

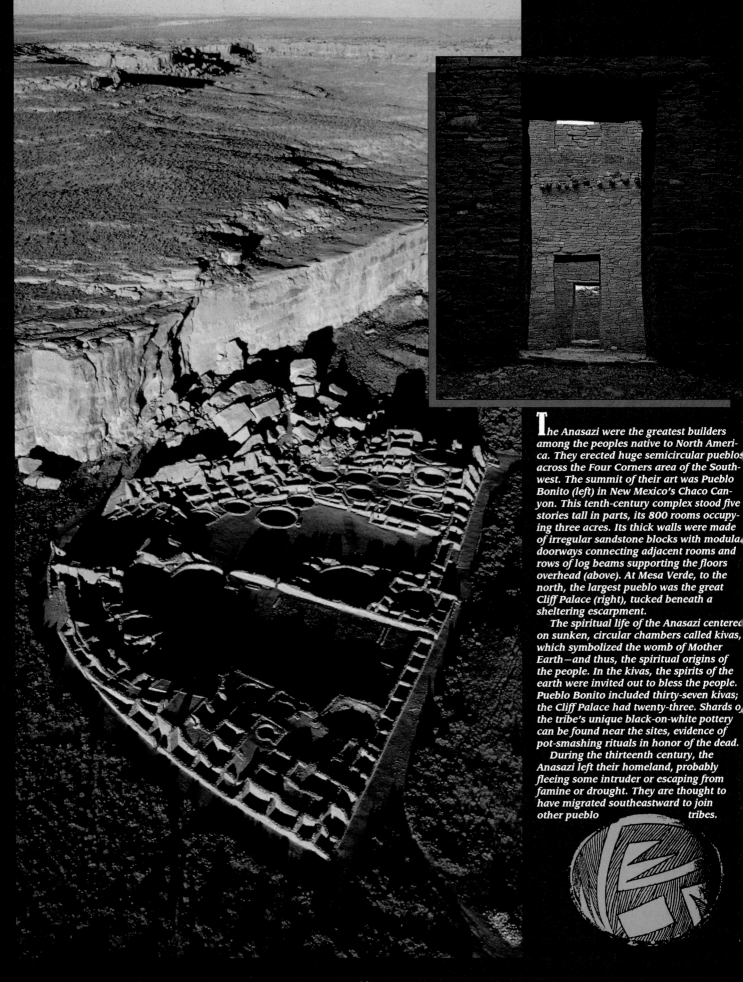

The Anasazi were the greatest builders among the peoples native to North America. They erected huge semicircular pueblos across the Four Corners area of the Southwest. The summit of their art was Pueblo Bonito (left) in New Mexico's Chaco Canyon. This tenth-century complex stood five stories tall in parts, its 800 rooms occupying three acres. Its thick walls were made of irregular sandstone blocks with modular doorways connecting adjacent rooms and rows of log beams supporting the floors overhead (above). At Mesa Verde, to the north, the largest pueblo was the great Cliff Palace (right), tucked beneath a sheltering escarpment.

The spiritual life of the Anasazi centered on sunken, circular chambers called kivas, which symbolized the womb of Mother Earth—and thus, the spiritual origins of the people. In the kivas, the spirits of the earth were invited out to bless the people. Pueblo Bonito included thirty-seven kivas; the Cliff Palace had twenty-three. Shards of the tribe's unique black-on-white pottery can be found near the sites, evidence of pot-smashing rituals in honor of the dead.

During the thirteenth century, the Anasazi left their homeland, probably fleeing some intruder or escaping from famine or drought. They are thought to have migrated southeastward to join other pueblo tribes.

CHAPTER 3

Enigmas of the Pacific

ver the centuries, the people of Easter Island have handed down a bittersweet legend about the circumstances under which their distant ancestors came to make a home on this harsh, lonely dot in the Pacific Ocean. The story has, no doubt, undergone minor changes, but its essence seems to have survived intact: The first settlers came from a continent called Hiva and a country known as Maori—the same name used today for the Polynesian natives of New Zealand. One day, a great cataclysm struck, and Hiva began to sink slowly into the sea.

King Hotu Matua, the powerful chieftain who ruled Maori, called together his people and told them they must abandon Hiva at once, before the waters engulfed them. The king and his followers embarked in two great canoes, faced with no choice but to search for a new home. After a treacherous journey lasting 120 days, they spotted a sandy, pink-hued beach on an uninhabited volcanic island. They named the place Te-Pito-o-te-Henua, or "navel of the world," and pushed their vessels ashore. That very day, Hotu Matua's wife gave birth to a boy, an event taken by all as a symbol of the new way of life that nature had imposed on the people of the lost continent.

Sunken lands also featured in another island legend about how the place came to have its present shape. According to that story, Easter Island used to be much larger than it is today. Long ago, however, a powerful deity named Uoke became violently enraged for reasons that are no longer known. He turned the Polynesian seas into a cauldron of storms, earthquakes, and volcanic eruptions. Then, armed with a gigantic lever, he stomped around the ocean prying loose every island that he found. Each one he heaved maliciously into the sea to be lost forever. When the god came to Easter Island, he was no less destructive, tearing away several large chunks of land. But the rocks of the island proved too sturdy for his lever, which broke before he could do away with the place altogether. Uoke departed, never to return, and Easter Island was saved from annihilation.

These tales of lands lost to the sea in great natural disasters or outpourings of divine ill humor are symptomatic, it seems clear, of the troubled past of the Easter Islanders. But the stories have also contributed to the speculation that many of the islands in the Pacific Ocean may be remnants of a former continent, which disappeared some 12,000 years ago. On a number of the islands in this part of the world, mysterious ruins and artifacts have turned up that feed such speculation. The discoveries suggest that the remote islands were once home to strange and forgotten cultures. Anthropologists, geologists, and archaeologists have begun recently to piece together a scientific understanding of the societies that developed in the Pacific and continue to explore the origins of the island dwellers. Much still remains to be learned, however, about these peoples and places.

The notion that the isles of the Pacific are the remains of a vast, lost continent first gained some measure of public attention in 1886, when an eccentric French physician and scholar, Augustus Le Plongeon, published his translation of what he claimed was a long-forgotten Mayan manuscript. He supposedly had discovered the writings while excavating some ruins on the Yucatán peninsula of Mexico. According to Le Plongeon's deciphering of the Mayan hieroglyphics contained in the manuscript, it told the extraordinary tale of the continent of Mu and the civilization that had thrived there. Le Plongeon professed to have evidence that the people of Mu were forebears not only of the Mayans but of the Egyptians as well.

In 1907, a prominent British archaeologist, Sir Aurel Stein, claimed to have discovered additional evidence of the existence of Mu. He reported that while working in a Tibetan desert village called Dunhuang, a Taoist monk had taken him to visit a hidden library within a mountain. Stein claimed that there he saw stacks of manuscripts that had been perfectly preserved for 800 years. He said the texts, some of which appeared to have been copied from even older manuscripts, were written in many languages, including Chinese, Tibetan, and Sanskrit. Several were in languages so obscure that Stein did not even recognize them. Among these latter manuscripts, he reported, was one that contained the fragments of a very old map, which showed a continent in the center of the Pacific Ocean.

Sir Aurel Stein was a noteworthy scholar, renowned for adventurous travels in support of his research. He wrote estimable works on such diverse subjects as the old China trade routes and the campaigns of Alexander the Great. But it must be said that he failed to provide a particularly satisfactory account of what became of his mysterious Tibetan map. Nor did he furnish any real guidance for historians wishing to pursue the matter further.

The doubtful but highly alluring concept of Mu rose to its peak of public popularity during the 1920s and 1930s, when James Churchward and Wishar Cervé published books about the vanished continent *(pages 8, 10)*. By that time, the mysterious land—known interchangeably as Mu, Lemuria, and Pacifica—had become the center of a genre of lost-continent theories that was nearly as rich as that of the fabled island of Atlantis.

Nevertheless, long before the alleged Pacific continent captured the imaginations of occultists, many Europeans were convinced that a great and mysterious southern continent existed somewhere in the relatively unexplored South Pacific. This belief first took root in 1687, when Edward Davis, a Dutch buccaneer commanding a British ship, sighted land in the Pacific where no European had ever reported it before. The land was mountainous, he said, and surrounded by a sandy atoll. Davis chose not to go ashore yet, however, for his ship had been fighting strong trade winds and powerful currents, and he was already far off course.

Thirty-five years later, the Dutch West India Company sent three sailing vessels under the command of Admiral Jacob Roggeveen to search for this once-spied landfall, which they referred to as Davis Land. After traveling thousands of miles over many weeks, and seeing little but unbroken blue seas and sky, Roggeveen and his men spotted a small volcanic island on the horizon. As the admiral recorded the event in his log, "There was great rejoicing among the people and everyone hoped that this low land might prove to be a foretoken of the coastline of the unknown Southern continent." It was Easter, 1722, and Roggeveen named the uncharted island in honor of the day.

With dusk descending, the three ships sailed closer to the isle, and Roggeveen and his crew could see columns of smoke rising from small fires on its cliffs. Whoever lived on the newly christened Easter Island had obviously spotted the ships and seemed to be signaling for the sailors to come ashore. Roggeveen decided, however, that it would be wiser to sleep on board and to wait until morning before venturing out to meet the islanders.

As luck would have it, the weather was foul for the next two days, and the waters were too rough for the ships to safely approach shore. But when dawn broke on the third morning and the Dutchmen sailed a little closer to the rocky beach, they were astounded by the scene they witnessed: Hundreds of people had prostrated themselves before the rising sun, the palms of their hands held together as if in prayer. And towering over the site of this ceremonial gathering were colossal stone statues, figures of some sort with their huge backs turned to the sea. On the heads of the statues

were cylindrical red stones, carved in what Roggeveen's men would later recognize as the shape of a topknot, or *pukao,* the traditional hair style of the island's men. "These stone figures caused us to be filled with wonder," Roggeveen would later write, "for we could not understand how it was possible that people who are destitute of heavy or thick timber, and also of stout cordage, out of which to construct gear, had been able to erect them." Some of the statues, he noted, were fully thirty feet tall.

Roggeveen sent a landing party ashore, and he discovered that he had been wise to be cautious about the islanders' response to their arrival. The reception was strangely mixed. Some islanders welcomed the sailors enthusiastically, while others seemed hostile and even began throwing stones. Frightened by the growing unruliness of the crowd on the beach, one of the sailors shouted, "It's time. It's time. Fire!" His comrades, unfortunately, complied with the order, and when the smoke from their muskets cleared, a dozen islanders lay dead. The others, naturally, fled. This tragic incident, which Roggeveen and his men genuinely seemed to regret, was an ominous harbinger of meetings to come between Dutchmen and the islanders.

The Europeans explored Easter Island for only

a day, finding that its inhabitants, whom they estimated to number about 5,000, led simple lives that bordered on poverty. All their tools were made of stone, and the islanders grew only three crops—sweet potatoes, bananas, and sugarcane. Roggeveen was surprised to observe that the people of this extremely isolated location seemed to be of two distinct ethnic groups. One group was tall and fair skinned, and many of its members had red hair. Known as the Hanau Eepe, or "long ears," these islanders got their name from the practice of wearing large ornamental wooden plugs in their earlobes, which had been stretched to accommodate the adornments. The other group was the Hanau Momoko,

From atop an ahu, or burial altar, seven colossal stone sentinels stand a quiet guard on Easter Island. These sixteen-ton giants are thought to honor the ancestors of the island's inhabitants. Although monolithic sculptures have been found on other Polynesian islands, the massive size and strange form of Easter Island's statues make them unique in the region.

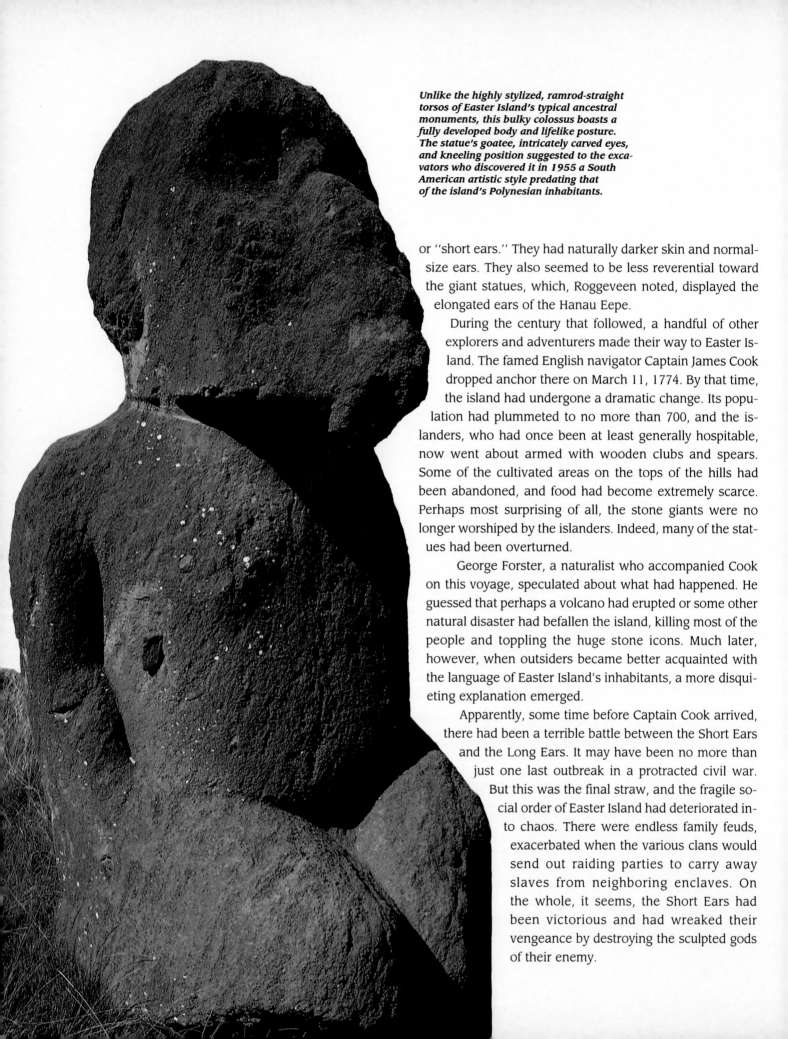

Unlike the highly stylized, ramrod-straight torsos of Easter Island's typical ancestral monuments, this bulky colossus boasts a fully developed body and lifelike posture. The statue's goatee, intricately carved eyes, and kneeling position suggested to the excavators who discovered it in 1955 a South American artistic style predating that of the island's Polynesian inhabitants.

or "short ears." They had naturally darker skin and normal-size ears. They also seemed to be less reverential toward the giant statues, which, Roggeveen noted, displayed the elongated ears of the Hanau Eepe.

During the century that followed, a handful of other explorers and adventurers made their way to Easter Island. The famed English navigator Captain James Cook dropped anchor there on March 11, 1774. By that time, the island had undergone a dramatic change. Its population had plummeted to no more than 700, and the islanders, who had once been at least generally hospitable, now went about armed with wooden clubs and spears. Some of the cultivated areas on the tops of the hills had been abandoned, and food had become extremely scarce. Perhaps most surprising of all, the stone giants were no longer worshiped by the islanders. Indeed, many of the statues had been overturned.

George Forster, a naturalist who accompanied Cook on this voyage, speculated about what had happened. He guessed that perhaps a volcano had erupted or some other natural disaster had befallen the island, killing most of the people and toppling the huge stone icons. Much later, however, when outsiders became better acquainted with the language of Easter Island's inhabitants, a more disquieting explanation emerged.

Apparently, some time before Captain Cook arrived, there had been a terrible battle between the Short Ears and the Long Ears. It may have been no more than just one last outbreak in a protracted civil war. But this was the final straw, and the fragile social order of Easter Island had deteriorated into chaos. There were endless family feuds, exacerbated when the various clans would send out raiding parties to carry away slaves from neighboring enclaves. On the whole, it seems, the Short Ears had been victorious and had wreaked their vengeance by destroying the sculpted gods of their enemy.

Although he was amazed by the design and workmanship of the statues, burial vaults, and other stone structures that he saw on Easter Island, James Cook found the natural setting of the place so desolate and its people so impoverished that he failed to see anything, short of dire distress, that could induce ships to put in at port on the island. "No nation," he wrote, "need contend for the honour of the discovery of this island, as there can be few places which afford less convenience for shipping than it does."

Despite Cook's dim assessment, ships continued to sail to Easter Island, and it was not until modern times that the consequences ceased to be tragic for the islanders. During the nineteenth century, they fell prey to slaving parties. The final and biggest of these raids occurred in 1862, when eighty armed men from eight Peruvian ships carried off nearly every able-bodied man and woman to labor in Peru. Among those taken was the island's king, Kaimakoi, along with his sons and daughters. Eventually, under pressure from the Catholic church, the Peruvian government ordered the return of the Easter Islanders, but before they could be repatriated to their homeland the majority had perished from smallpox or from the many other hardships of their life abroad. The fifteen freed slaves who did manage to return to the island brought the smallpox virus with them. And by 1877, the island's population had dwindled to 111 destitute souls.

After Easter Island

Despite their irregular shapes, the big basalt blocks that form Easter Island's Ahu Tahira platform abut perfectly with one another. To create tight seams without mortar, islanders chipped the surfaces to a precise fit—a technique reminiscent of classical Inca masonry.

was annexed by Chile in 1888, life was somewhat improved for the islanders. The slave raids came to an end, and the majority of foreigners who now visited were either peaceful missionaries or scientists drawn to the island by the puzzle of its great statues. Compiling a comprehensive history of Easter Island and its carvings would prove to be a difficult task, however. Much of the knowledge regarding old customs or veneration of the statues had been lost forever when King Kaimakoi and the other elders of the island perished as a result of the slave raids. These captives were the last of the islanders who had been initiated in the ancient secrets of the place.

What can be determined about the stone gods is that they were sculpted from the hardened lava of Rano Raraku, one of the island's three extinct volcanoes. About 600 of the carvings survive. They were made, apparently, to honor the dead, and many were placed on great stone funeral platforms known as ahus. Other statues were scattered across the grasslands and volcanic slopes of the island in a seemingly random pattern that has perplexed many observers. "During the three weeks we lived among the statues, we saw them in sunshine, by moonlight, and on stormy nights," wrote Alfred Métraux, a member of a 1934 French expedition to Easter Island. "Each time we felt the same shock, the same uneasiness, as on the first day. This sense of oppression is due less to their dimen-

sions than to their confused distribution. If they were arranged in some apparent order one could catch a glimpse of the purpose and plan of the dead; but the almost human casualness and turbulence with which this assembly of giants with huge noses and flat necks is scattered about is somehow disturbing."

The statues vary greatly in height, but the majority range from twelve to twenty-five feet, and the largest is thirty-seven feet tall. They weigh as much as fifty tons. Even larger carvings, including one enormous image sixty-six feet long, lie in various stages of completion in the quarry. A variety of tools were also abandoned at the quarry site, leading scientists to speculate that the sculptors halted their work quite abruptly. Some of the sociologists who have studied Easter Island believe that the sudden end of statue construction may have been caused by the revolt of the Short Ears and the ensuing civil war.

Island folklore, however, offers a more exotic explanation for the mysterious cessation of statue building. According to a popular legend, a sorceress who cooked for the workmen in the Rano Raraku quarry became enraged when some of her food disappeared while she was away visiting relatives. She vented her anger by casting a spell on the statues, causing those that were already standing to topple and those being created in the quarry to remain forever in an unfinished state.

Whatever the reason for the abrupt end of statue building, the most puzzling questions about the completed stone giants are how they were transported from the quarry to their present sites and how they were raised to standing positions. Over the years, scientists and would-be archaeological detectives have offered many different explanations; they range from quite-plausible wooden rollers and sleds to aerial tramways that require a stretch of the imagination. One investigator declared that the statues were not moved by humans at all but were carried by lava flows during the island's many volcanic eruptions.

During a scientific expedition to Easter Island in 1956, Norwegian archaeologist and adventurer Thor Heyerdahl helped resolve part of the mystery. At Heyerdahl's request, a group of islanders agreed to demonstrate the techniques their ancestors used to erect the giant statues. "Twelve men toiled for eighteen days to get the twenty-ton giant back up on top of the ahu where it had formerly stood," Heyerdahl later wrote. "They used nothing but their muscles, poles, and a quantity of stones. By prying up first one side and then the other in jerks that resulted in almost invisible movements of the giant, they put progressively larger stones underneath it, until the colossus lay on top of a huge stone pile taller than they were. Then they transferred their activity to the image's head, building up more piles of stones under the face and shoulders until the [statue] tilted on end of its own weight and stood gazing out over our camp with deep empty eye sockets."

But when Heyerdahl pressed for an explanation of how the statues were moved from the quarry, the Easter Islanders said that was simple: The stone giants had walked by themselves. No tools or human effort was needed, explained the islanders. The statues had been charged with an ancient supernatural force called mana. This was the source of life, power, and death. It was associated with a variety of objects on the island, but especially with the great stone carvings.

Unconvinced by the supernatural explanations put forth by his volunteers, Heyerdahl persuaded them to test a more worldly theory of his own. In the course of his research, he had learned that the early inhabitants of Easter Island had used a sort of forked-pole sled to carry smaller stones from place to place. He thought it very likely they had used a similar device in moving the multiton statues. After constructing a replica of a pole sled, Heyerdahl and 180 volunteers used it to drag a fallen twelve-ton statue across a sandy beach. Although the experiment required a tremendous amount of physical effort, it proved that the statues could have been moved in such a manner—at least across a beach. But the colossal carvings had somehow traversed a much more daunting route, down the slopes of a volcano. Heyerdahl recorded that the mayor and elders of

the island "insisted that according to their ancestors the statues had not been dragged but had walked erect."

Other investigators have suggested an explanation for the legend of the walking statues. They conjecture that the massive stones might have yielded most easily to muscle power if they were first turned upright, then rocked from side to side while at the same time being pulled forward with a rope. A solitary worker can move a heavy refrigerator this way, and it is conceivable that the same technique might have been applied to the gigantic, top-heavy stones. If the carvings were indeed transported in this manner, then it becomes immediately obvious where the impression of "walking" statues arose.

Although Easter Island's strange and sullen statues have attracted a great deal of attention worldwide, they are not the only mysterious artifacts that sprang from this culture. Even more perplexing, in the view of some scientists, are the so-called talking boards, sacred wooden tablets inscribed with an as yet undeciphered script known as rongorongo. According to island folklore, King Hotu Matua brought sixty-seven of the tablets with him when he first settled the island. The talking boards were said to contain ancient proverbs, traditions, stories, and genealogical records. They were considered so sacred that the penalty for touching them was death. Knowledge of the tablets was handed down from generation to generation, but only within a few select families. Once a year, during a great feast, these privileged few would recite the contents of the tablets for the benefit of the other islanders.

Unfortunately, all those capable of interpreting the rongorongo markings perished during the slave raids of the nineteenth century or in the smallpox epidemic that followed. By the time historians became aware of the tablets, there was no one left who could decipher them. Some modern experts who have examined these relics believe the characters on them do not represent a system of writing but are instead pictographs meant to jog the memory of the readers. Each pictograph symbolized a key element of a

Bringing Dreams and Theories to Life

"I am a very realistic person," said Thor Heyerdahl, the Norwegian explorer whose voyages tested ideas about ancient travel that others thought completely unrealistic. "All my work is based on fact and sustained by fact."

Not the facts one might find in a book, it seems, but those experienced and proved firsthand. Even as a child, Heyerdahl was convinced that people relied too much on the opinions and impressions of others. He was determined to see life as it really was.

Heyerdahl, born in 1914, showed an early love for the natural world. He collected bats, butterflies, and other biological specimens, and as a teenager he became an avid outdoorsman. Only then did he share with trusted friends his dream of living close to nature. His vision of paradise, which he had illustrated at the tender age of eight *(right)*, waited somewhere in the mysterious South Seas. He vowed to become an explorer and find it; at age twenty-two he completed the first leg of a lifelong journey when he and his new wife, Liv, landed in Polynesia.

A young Thor Heyerdahl displays his trophies from a weekend fishing trip—several trout and a live duck. Heyerdahl was greatly influenced by a hermit he met one summer, who schooled the boy in wilderness skills and a back-to-nature philosophy.

Experiencing some aspects of nature that perhaps were not part of his boyhood dreams, Heyerdahl (left) returns from an absence of only a few weeks to find his cabin on the South Seas island of Fatu Hiva caving in and the jungle quickly restaking its claim. While in Polynesia, he became fascinated with the ancient mysteries shrouding those islands—including the origin of the inhabitants. True to his belief that the proof is in the doing, Heyerdahl tested his theory that the Polynesians could have come from South America by re-creating a migratory voyage. He and four companions built a primitive forty-foot balsa-log raft (right), naming it Kon-Tiki for a storied Peruvian king said to have sailed west to the islands centuries earlier on such a vessel. Heyerdahl and his crew completed their trip in 101 adventure-filled days.

Believing that supernatural powers had sent Heyerdahl to them, an Easter Island couple presented these "holy, serious stones" to the explorer when he visited in 1955. Symbolizing guardian spirits, or akuakus, the carved stones vary in design and purpose: The skull was considered the key to a secret entrance in the family cave, where such objects are traditionally hidden; the long-eared figure resembles the giant statues thought to guard the island; and the carving of a three-masted boat may commemorate early seafarers. The couple's gifts to Heyerdahl ceased when the wife sensed she had angered the akuakus by depleting the cave's contents.

proverb or story memorized and passed on orally by generations of readers. It may never be possible, therefore, to recover the information solely on the basis of the pictographs.

In 1932, the Belgian linguist Guillaume de Hevesy stirred up a controversy among language scholars when he reported that there were significant similarities between the symbols on Easter Island's rongorongo tablets and the symbols used by people in the Indus Valley some 5,000 years ago. In fact, de Hevesy claimed, so many of the symbols were identical that it was unlikely the similarities could be attributed to coincidence.

Surprisingly, other scholars have raised the possibility of connections between the customs of Easter Island and those of ancient Indian civilizations. Thor Heyerdahl, for one, noted that the oldest known practice of ear extension was found among the seamen of Lothal, once a bustling port for travelers to and from the Indus Valley. Apparently, these mariners wore earplugs that were nearly identical to those used by the Long Ears on Easter Island. French explorer and oceanographer Philippe Cousteau, who toured the South Pacific in 1976, noted similarities between the songs of Easter Island and those of India. He also pointed out that the islanders once routinely cremated their dead, until wood became too scarce. Cremation is still a common practice among the Hindus of India.

The possibility that a system of pictographs and various cultural practices may have spread from India to the South Pacific raises once again the most prickly question concerning Easter Island: Where did its original inhabitants come from? It is an extremely isolated place. The nearest inhabited land to the west, some 1,200 miles away, is Pitcairn Island, which was made famous by the perpetrators of a celebrated mutiny involving the British ship *Bounty*. To the east, the closest land is the coast of Chile, some 2,000 miles away. For people to travel such huge distances in the fourth century AD—roughly the time when the first settlers probably reached Easter Island—would have required superb seamanship and boatbuilding skills.

Regardless of the native legends about Hiva and Hotu Matua, the prevailing theory among scholars today is that the first settlers on Easter Island were island-hopping Polynesians who had come originally from Southeast Asia. According to this view, the immigrants arrived in formidable twin-hull canoes that were capable of traveling great distances at sea. In the 1940s, Thor Heyerdahl proposed an alternative theory that attracted a good deal of attention, although it has since lost most of its adherents.

Heyerdahl believed that Easter Island, and possibly the rest of the South Pacific, was discovered and settled by people sailing westward from South America. He presumed that the ancient cities of Peru were the most likely points of embarkation. And in 1947, Heyerdahl set out to prove that the Peruvians of pre-Inca times had the capability of sailing to faraway islands. He and five companions launched a small balsa raft, christened *Kon-Tiki,* and floated some 4,300 nautical miles from the coast of Peru to the Polynesian atoll of Raroia. The journey took 101 days.

Relying heavily on centuries-old legends as well as on archaeological and anthropological evidence, Thor Heyerdahl has proposed that Easter Island was, in all likelihood, peopled twice. The first settlers came from Peru. These were the Long Ears, light-skinned and red-haired, who worshiped their ancestors by hoisting giant stone sculptures into place. Some indeterminate number of generations later, the dark-skinned Short Ears arrived from the west. They came in peace and accepted most of the Long Ears' customs. After about 200 years, the Short Ears revolted—perhaps because they were tired of slaving away for the benefit of the Long Ears—and thus began the terrible era known as *huri moai,* or "overthrowing of the statues." Cannibalism became a common practice, and many of the great statues were destroyed. It was during this violent and destructive period that the first Europeans arrived.

Wherever they originated, the people who settled Easter Island and the other 25,000 or so islands in the Pacific long ago created a variety of strange, megalithic monuments and other curiosities that have mystified scientists and historians ever since. For example, on the Isle of Pines—a small, tree-covered islet located thirty-two miles south of New Caledonia—archaeologists have uncovered some 400 anthill-shaped mounds of gravel and sand called tumuli. The mounds average about 8 feet in height and 300 feet in diameter. Archaeologists have never been sure why they were constructed, and the mystery surrounding them deepened in the early 1960s, when several of the tumuli were found to contain upright pillars.

The columns were made of a lime-mortar compound, mixed with bits of broken shells. When scientists measured their age with the radiocarbon-dating process, the pillars were found to be 7,000 to 13,000 years old. Naturally, the great age of these peculiar monuments was music to the ears of lost-continent theorists, and at least one writer seized upon the find as evidence that the mounds may have been landing pads for ancient astronauts. Conventional archaeologists are still seeking down-to-earth explanations for the mounds.

The Kiribati Islands, a remote group of sixteen islands on the equator in the western reaches of the Pacific Ocean, are home to several monuments that are every bit as strange as the tumuli. On one richly vegetated islet there is a circle of earth in which no plants are able to grow. The circle is forty-four feet in diameter and has at its center a sixteen-foot square outlined with small oblong stones. The islanders claim the circle is guarded by an ancient spirit. They never enter its perimeter, for doing so, they believe, is tantamount to suicide.

On another Kiribati island, investigators discovered the fifteen-foot-long graves of two supposed giants who, according to island legend, originally came from the sky. The giants were said to be brothers and to possess superhuman strength. The islanders lived in fear of this daunting pair and thus conspired to kill them after first getting them thoroughly drunk. Once this double murder was carried out, the bodies of the giants were placed in deep graves, which were filled up with heavy stones. One of the tombs has since been covered over to make room for the construc-

tion of a community center; the other can still be seen.

Stories of giants also circulate in relation to another curious feature on the Kiribati Islands—huge footprints preserved in volcanic stone on the capital island of Tarawa. The massive prints, measuring three feet in length, are located in an area known as *Te Aba-n-Anti*, or "place of the spirits." They seem to have been left by some strange crea-

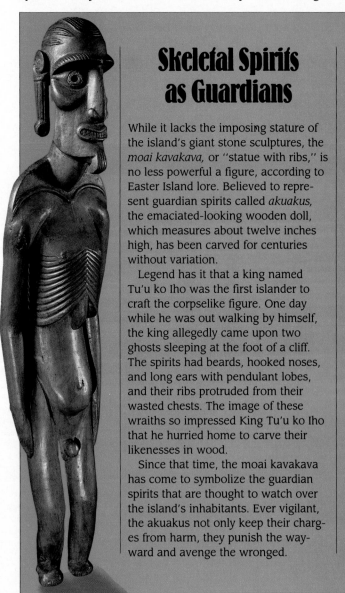

Skeletal Spirits as Guardians

While it lacks the imposing stature of the island's giant stone sculptures, the *moai kavakava*, or "statue with ribs," is no less powerful a figure, according to Easter Island lore. Believed to represent guardian spirits called *akuakus*, the emaciated-looking wooden doll, which measures about twelve inches high, has been carved for centuries without variation.

Legend has it that a king named Tu'u ko Iho was the first islander to craft the corpselike figure. One day while he was out walking by himself, the king allegedly came upon two ghosts sleeping at the foot of a cliff. The spirits had beards, hooked noses, and long ears with pendulant lobes, and their ribs protruded from their wasted chests. The image of these wraiths so impressed King Tu'u ko Iho that he hurried home to carve their likenesses in wood.

Since that time, the moai kavakava has come to symbolize the guardian spirits that are thought to watch over the island's inhabitants. Ever vigilant, the akuakus not only keep their charges from harm, they punish the wayward and avenge the wronged.

ture with six toes on each foot. According to island legend, the footprints were made by a giant called Tabuariki, whose great height enabled him to pluck coconuts from the tallest palm trees without even stretching his arms. He, too, was said to have come to the island from the clouds.

The folklore of the Kiribati Islands contains many other tales of gods descending from the sky. In fact, the islanders have two names for the different types of beings on the earth: *Aomata* means simply "man," while *te i-matang* distinguishes a "man from land of the gods." This distinction has led some observers—most notably, Swiss occultist and author Erich von Däniken, who spent time in Kiribati during 1980—to suggest that these remote bits of land in the Pacific were once visited by ancient space travelers. It has even been proposed that a collection of large vertical stones found on the island of Arorae may have provided compass bearings to astronauts high above, directing them to specific islands hundreds of miles away.

Other islands scattered throughout the Pacific are home to large stone megaliths, whose ancient purposes may never be completely understood. Many centuries ago, the inhabitants of one of the islands of Tonga, for example, built a lofty arch from three massive slabs of coral limestone. Some early writers believed that this structure—known traditionally as the Ha'amonga of Maui, or "burden of the god Maui"—figured in the rituals of an ancient sun-worshiping cult.

According to one tradition, the people who built the Ha'amonga of Maui took their stoneworking skills to the island of Pohnpei, where they built the citylike complex of Nan Madol—one of the most mysterious and remarkable archaeological sites in the world. Pohnpei was formerly called Ponape, and before that Ascension Island. It is a lush, volcanic bit of land situated seven degrees north of the equator in the eastern part of the Caroline Islands. Turn-of-the-century scholars believed that Pohnpei may have been the capital of a great Pacific empire at one time.

The ruined city of Nan Madol is sometimes called the Venice of the Pacific. It encompasses about seven square miles of abandoned buildings, many of them standing on nearly 100 artificial islets. The islets are separated by narrow canals and thus resemble small city blocks. All of the city's structures, from the foundations of the islets to the houses, temples, and feast halls, were built with column-shaped pieces of basalt that were used like logs. The stones were quarried from an island, roughly five miles away, just off the north coast of Pohnpei. No one knows for certain how the heavy stones—some of them weigh as much as twenty-five tons—were transported from the island to Nan Madol. The local folklore suggests that rafts were used, a seemingly reasonable explanation.

Nan Madol seems to have been carefully planned, with each islet serving a particular purpose. One islet, called Karian, was the official burial site for the city's priests. *Ketieu* plants, long believed to dispel ghosts, still grow on Karian today. Another islet, known as Idehd, was the city's

By the eighteenth century, Nan Madol was already so thoroughly swallowed up by jungle foliage that the European explorers who stopped at Pohnpei did not even make note of the ruined city. The best-known early description of Nan Madol was written by an Irishman named James O'Connell, who was shipwrecked on the island in 1826. Three chiefs vied for control of Pohnpei at that time, and clan warfare was common. The quick-witted O'Connell managed to save his own life by ingratiating himself with one of the chiefs. Supposedly, he did so by performing many versions of the Irish jig and by permitting the islanders to cover his white skin with tattoos. The chief became so taken with the foreigner that he offered his own fourteen-year-old daughter as a wife. O'Connell accepted readily and settled into island life, eventually fathering two sons by the young bride. The Irishman would remain on Pohnpei until 1837, when he was rescued by a passing ship.

The rescued sailor wrote a book about his sojourn in the South Seas, *A Residence of Eleven Years in New Holland and the Caroline Islands: Being the Adventures of James O'Connell.* In this memoir he included an account of a visit to Nan Madol. It seems that he must have used every bit of his charm and persuasive abilities to get permission to tour the ruins, for the islanders considered the city taboo and shunned it as infested with ghosts and evil spirits. For his part, O'Connell was clearly awed by the lost city, which he summed up as being "the most stupendous ruins of a character of architecture differing altogether from the recent style of the islanders, and of an extent truly astonishing."

Many visitors have followed O'Connell to Nan Madol, both as tourists and as scholars hoping to solve the riddles posed by the ruins. One of the first scientists to explore the island was German-Pole Johann Stanislaus Kubary, a talented and influential archaeologist, whose personal life was more than a little chaotic. Kubary was married to four women, each from a different island. One of the wives hailed from Pohnpei. Kubary conducted excavations in Nan Madol during the 1870s, but all the artifacts that he discovered were tragically lost at sea, when the ship on which the

religious center. This area featured an underwater tunnel through which large eels were enticed into a special pool to play a part in religious rites. Oral tradition relates that the local religion called for sea turtles to be sacrificed each year during a particular ceremony. The dead turtles were baked, and a portion of the meat was fed to the eels, while a priest asked for forgiveness from the gods.

Many people who see Nan Madol firsthand find that the experience can be both awe-inspiring and slightly unnerving. "Visiting the city is a shocking experience," wrote novelist and screenwriter Bill Ballinger. "It is hidden from the air and not visible from land or sea. Nan Madol lies beneath a thick canopy of towering trees and is entirely camouflaged by a thick, interlocking, rapacious undergrowth of jungle brush, bushes, weeds, vines, and moss. The great walls have been wrecked by the thrusting roots of the giant trees, and the cannibalistic appetite of the jungle gnaws away at the skeleton remains." Ballinger is convinced that in terms of sheer mass of materials transported, Nan Madol was surpassed only by the Great Wall of China and, possibly, by the pyramids of Egypt.

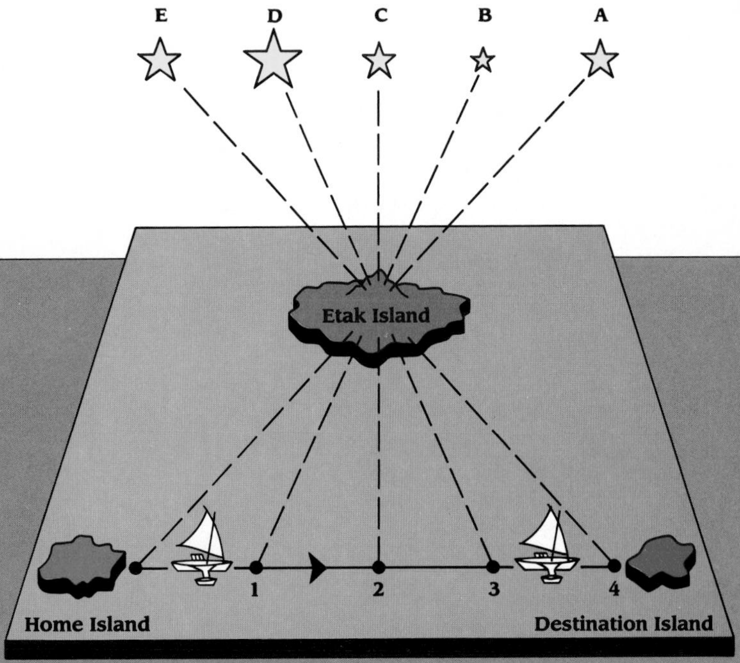

E   D   C   B   A

Etak Island

Home Island   Destination Island

1   2   3   4

As explained by David Lewis, author of We, the Navigators, some Pacific explorers used etak, or reference islands, to chart a course from one point to another and to measure the distance traveled. An etak island was chosen for its known position between two points, as shown in the diagram at right. Every navigator memorized the position of the stars and which islands lay beneath them, so he knew from the outset under which star the etak island appeared to rest when visualized from the home island—here, the etak island lies beneath star A. As the canoe moves from the home island toward its destination, the etak island seems to travel backward, first to star B, then to star C, and so on; from the destination island, the etak appears to rest beneath star E. To measure a journey's distance, each apparent movement backward by the etak island—from star A to star B, for example—was said to equal one etak; the journey diagramed here would measure four etaks.

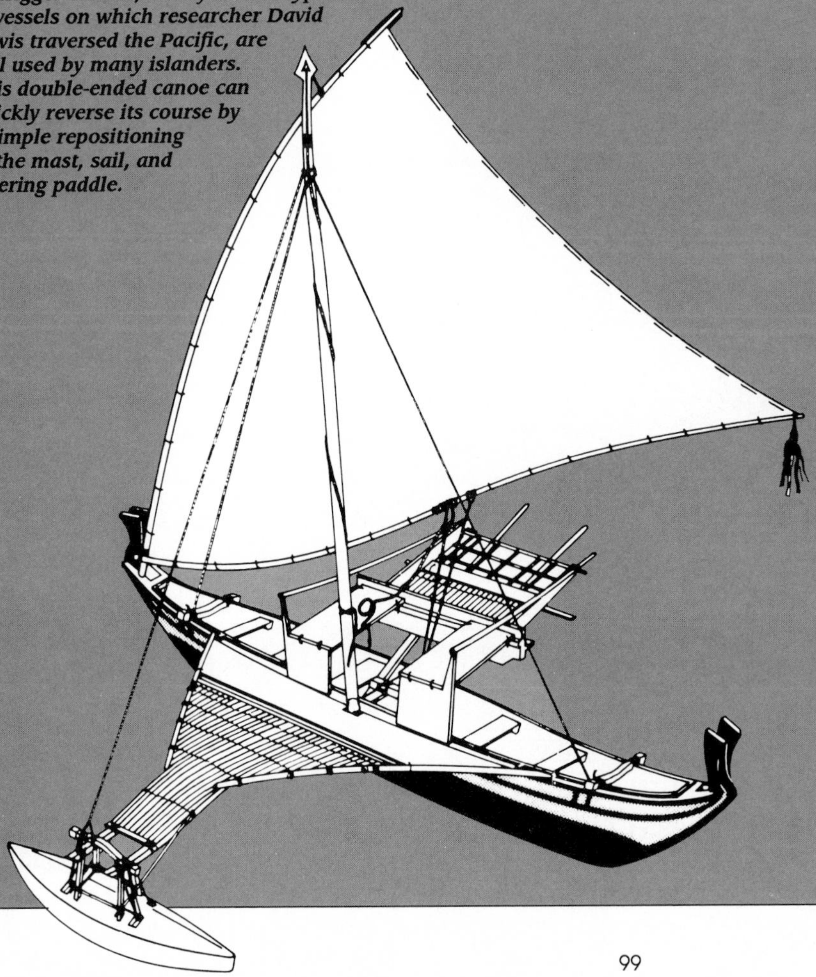

Outrigger canoes, one of several types of vessels on which researcher David Lewis traversed the Pacific, are still used by many islanders. This double-ended canoe can quickly reverse its course by a simple repositioning of the mast, sail, and steering paddle.

The Demanding Art of Island Navigation

When European explorers first sailed the Pacific in the 1500s, they found that every habitable speck of land had been settled by the Polynesians. In fact, in the centuries between about 2500 BC and AD 800, those intrepid voyagers spread themselves throughout some 15 million square miles of uncharted ocean.

Just how they made such long journeys out of sight of land without even rudimentary navigational devices remained a mystery until 1968, when New Zealand yachtsman David Lewis began studying the question. He explored the Pacific with islanders who had been trained from boyhood to read the wind, waves, and currents and to detect unseen land over the horizon from such signs as the flight patterns of birds and cloud formations. But most important, they had memorized a vast amount of astronomical and geographical data, including the year-round positions of stars and of the islands that lie beneath them.

treasures were being carried had a mishap and sank some-where near the Marshall Islands. Several years later, Kubary committed suicide, apparently after learning that his Pohnpei wife had taken another husband. Kubary left behind an unpublished manuscript about the history of Nan Madol, but it, too, was lost—in a fire during the 1930s.

In the years since Kubary's lifetime, archaeologists have learned a great deal about Nan Madol, yet there is still no consensus about when the place was built. Some scholars believe that the city was constructed around AD 900; a

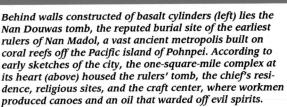

Behind walls constructed of basalt cylinders (left) lies the Nan Douwas tomb, the reputed burial site of the earliest rulers of Nan Madol, a vast ancient metropolis built on coral reefs off the Pacific island of Pohnpei. According to early sketches of the city, the one-square-mile complex at its heart (above) housed the rulers' tomb, the chief's residence, religious sites, and the craft center, where workmen produced canoes and an oil that warded off evil spirits.

Map labels:
Tomb of Saudeleurs (Nan Douwas)
North
Craft Center
Priest's Burial Site (Karian)
Turtle Altar
Chief's Residence
Turtle Sacrifice Area (Idehd)

stone city has probably been around for a much longer time—perhaps 1,500 years or more. Ayres suggests that Nan Madol was most likely abandoned sometime in the fifteenth century. Various writers have proposed that the cause of this desertion was an earthquake, an epidemic, or a tribal war; island tradition supports the idea that the cause was some sort of civil unrest.

Many legends exist about the identity of Nan Madol's founders. One story suggests that the city was built by two brothers named Olsihpa and Olsohpa. They paddled to Pohnpei in a canoe, arriving from a distant land, and quickly assumed control of the island. They persuaded the inhabitants to build a temple and an impressive new seat of government. Eventually, after erecting several smaller structures in various parts of the island, the brothers set to work on the great city of Nan Madol. By that time, however, they had acquired wondrous magic powers. Making use of special chants and prayers, they caused the thousands of basalt logs to fly through the air with such great speed and precision that the city was completed in a single day.

The story of Olsihpa and Olsohpa does not end there. According to the folklore of Pohnpei, the brothers governed the island jointly until Olsihpa died, then the surviving brother ascended the throne as the first *saudeleur*, or

few are vehemently certain that it is no older than the seventeenth century and may be even more recent than that. Anthropologist William Ayres of the University of Oregon, who has been studying Nan Madol since 1977, is one of a growing number of researchers who are convinced that the "chief," of the island. Olsohpa and the fifteen saudeleurs who succeeded him reigned in peace over Pohnpei for the next twelve generations. The era of tranquillity came to an end, at last, when a warrior chief named Isokelekel invaded the island and founded a new line of monarchs. The Nahnmwarkis, as these chiefs were called, have held sway into modern times.

Yet another island tale reveals that Nan Madol was built by a race of very small people, who were said to be as violent as they were clever. According to the legend, the dwarfs possessed supernatural powers that were every bit the match for the skills of Olsihpa and Olsohpa. Long after Nan Madol was deserted, the people of Pohnpei feared the dwarfs, who were said still to haunt the mountains and forests of the island.

At the turn of the twentieth century some anthropologists believed that the tales of a pygmy race on Pohnpei may have had historical merit. These writers suggested that people of diminutive stature were the earliest inhabitants of Melanesia, the large group of islands just to the south of Pohnpei. And the scholars deduced that pygmies may very well have been the original inhabitants of Pohnpei as well— and thus could have been the visionaries behind the construction of Nan Madol. Support for such a theory has all but vanished, however, as more has been learned about the history of the Pacific races.

Island legend also makes room for some tall people on Pohnpei—supposedly after the dwarfs had vanished into the mountains. In 1928, an excavation by Japanese archaeologists uncovered very large human bones in some of Nan Madol's tombs. According to the Japanese investigators, the remains proved that people as tall as seven feet once inhabited the island. No one knows for certain where such lanky islanders might have come from, but one possibility is Tonga. Historically, the people of Tonga were quite large by South Pacific standards. Moreover, there is a legend on that island that claims a connection with Nan Madol.

Ruins similar to those of Nan Madol can be found on Kosrae, another volcanic island, about 300 miles east of Pohnpei. The Kosrae ruins, however, are much less extensive and somewhat more crudely constructed. Many of the people of Nan Madol believe the Kosrae structures may have been built by workmen from their island and used as an outpost of some kind. Not surprisingly, the inhabitants of Kosrae take precisely the opposite view. There are few clues that would seem to link the two islands. Although the stone architecture of Pohnpei and Kosrae is similar, their languages are quite different. Archaeologists are still trying to sort out which island was settled first and why. One myth does connect them: It is said that Isokelekel, the warlike chief who invaded Pohnpei and overthrew the saudeleurs, sailed originally from Kosrae.

Other island legends also tell of two sunken cities near Nan Madol. Both are said to have great underground gates or entrances guarded by two female spirits. Islanders also speak of fishermen who in recent times have speared sea turtles, which then towed them down to the underwater cities. "One such fisherman reported seeing a wall in the deep channel," reported Arthur Saxe, a government consultant who surveyed Nan Madol in 1980. "He bled to death," Saxe related, "from the compression of the depth shortly after relating the story."

Saxe commissioned divers to search for the remains of the sunken cities, and—according to his report—they made an astonishing discovery. "Our findings verify the existence of coral-encrusted formations in the deep channel that are unusual and may provide a factual base for the stories, especially the columns and the straight line of boulders," Saxe wrote. "If the patterning fits with linear surface features as we suspect, then these may well be artifactual. More investigations will of course be necessary before explanations can be made."

Such findings only deepen the mystery surrounding Nan Madol and the other strange ruins in the South Pacific. Whether they are traces of lost civilizations or simply the remains of primitive cultures long since disappeared, they continue to perplex scientists and historians alike, as they have done for centuries.

Looking at the 2,000-year-old carvings above, it is easy to imagine the artists who shaped them chatting companionably under a shade tree. Yet the bearded elder at left was made in what is now Costa Rica, while the figure at right was fashioned in China—more than 5,000 miles away.

Most scholars dismiss the resemblance between such Asian and American artifacts as coincidence; the objects, they say, are parallel products of cultures at the same stage of development. But for so-called diffusionists, that explanation is not enough. Citing thousands of strikingly similar myths, customs, and works of art from both sides of the Pacific, these researchers argue that Asian sailors must have reached the New World millennia ago, "diffusing" Chinese and Japanese ideas into the cultures of their American hosts. Others, albeit few bearing academic credentials, propose even more startling explanations—suggesting the similarities are evidence that a lost continent once bridged the Pacific *(page 7)*.

In these pages, a sampling of ancient artifacts from both continents suggests the uncanny likenesses that fuel this dispute. "Each of us must decide," mythologist Joseph Campbell wrote, "whether to believe it possible that the human mind might be programmed in such detail that through the interfacing simply of the psyche and a landscape such a multitude of correspondences could have evolved."

With a ferocious smile much like that of the ancient Chinese dragon sculpture at right, an image of the Teotihuacán serpent god emerges from a gold ornament (left) made in Central America nine to twelve centuries ago. In their respective cultures, both of the toothed reptiles were considered benevolent deities; both symbolized strength, wisdom, and the marriage of earth and spirit.

Elaborately incised designs adorn a jaguar-
shaped Andean mortar (left) carved as early
as 700 BC. Such designs are also found on a
jade Chinese tiger (right) fashioned between
770 and 221 BC. Both the American jaguar
and the Asian tiger were worshiped by cults
and associated with shamanistic power.

Emanating serenity, the Mayan deity at left
meditates within a lily as though in deliberate mimicry of the classic Chinese Buddha
enthroned at right upon a lotus flower.

At far left, a seventh- or eighth-century carving of the Mayan corn god lifts one palm and lowers the other in a gesture that some scholars interpret as reassuring. In a nearly identical pose, the sixth-century gilded bronze Buddha at left raises one hand in a gesture meaning "Fear not," while his other hand signals that a wish has been granted.

Three-legged ceramic pots like the one at left served as everyday cookware in Ecuador between 1,000 and 500 years ago. Diffusionists argue that the tripod design may have been inspired by Chinese cooking vessels like the Stone Age example at right.

At left, a clay architectural model from the coast of Ecuador depicts a house of that region perhaps 1,500 years ago. Its steep, rain-shedding roof, unnecessary in the arid Peruvian climate, curiously resembles those on the sculpted buildings atop the jar at right, made in China between AD 265 and 316.

Stylized Andean villagers join hands for a circle dance around the rim of this earthenware plate, made in pre-Columbian Ecuador sometime between AD 500 and 1500. At far right, similar stick figures grace a Chinese bowl thought to have been fashioned three to five thousand years before the plate.

Patterns of spirals ornament both the burnished clay bottle at left, a product of the ancient Chavin culture of the Andes, and the earlier Chinese cooking pot at right. Lines on the bottle are thought to form a stylized cat; those on the pot are said by scholars to represent a series of winged dragons.

The grimace of the Peruvian god (left), fashioned by members of the jaguar cult between 200 BC and AD 800, bears more than a passing resemblance to traditional Japanese images of the god of death such as the one at right. In addition to feline fangs and bulging eyes, each figure incorporates a headdress with a likeness of its own face.

CHAPTER 4

Before Columbus Arrived

**M**ost children in the United States still dutifully learn that Christopher Columbus discovered America in 1492. The Italian-born navigator, who sailed under the flag of the king and queen of Spain, is a cultural icon in the United States. His birthday is a national holiday, and his story is recalled in school pageants and nursery rhymes. This is certainly justified, since the famous mariner's first voyage across the Atlantic was enormously influential in opening the eyes of Europe to the rich frontiers on the other side of the sea. But the continuing adulation bestowed on Columbus is also somewhat curious, for there is now ample reason to believe that other Old World explorers preceded him to America.

The Vikings, another name that looms large in the imaginations of schoolchildren, almost certainly came before him. And according to a diverse band of revisionist historians, there may have been many others—a steady stream, in fact, of explorers, traders, and colony builders who journeyed to America from a variety of ports over a period of several millennia.

China is a nation not often associated with New World exploration. Yet studies of a book called the *Shan-hai ching,* one of the oldest treatises on geography, have led a few of the radical historians to assert that the Chinese probably crisscrossed North America more than 4,000 years ago.

The scholars who make this claim base their hypothesis on a section of the *Shan-hai ching* called *The Classic of Eastern Mountains.* In that disquisition, the authors provided detailed physical descriptions of several dozen mountains. Some readers, over the centuries, dismissed the work as a study of geomancy rather than a discussion of science or geography. Tall peaks, after all, had long figured in Oriental traditions of magic as great repositories of earth energy. Be that as it may, the mountains described in the book were said to be situated "beyond the Eastern Sea," and a number of latter-day historians seized on the phrase as a reference to the Pacific Ocean.

Fortunately for them, the *Shan-hai ching* authors had included descriptions of their travels among the various mountains they discussed. In doing so, they provided useful data such as distances and directions that allowed the historians to re-create—or, at least, so those scholars would claim—the itineraries of four extended geographical survey missions carried out many centuries ago. According to these interpretations, the Chinese explorers ranged far and wide between the present-day Canadian province of Manitoba and the northern regions of Mexico.

There are problems with this theory, of course. Most troublesome is that its central inspiration—the venerable *Shan-hai ching*—is a controversial work. Although the book is certainly quite old, dating it is anything but straightforward. For centuries it was attributed to the emperor Yu, a quasi-mythological figure said to have ascended the Chinese throne in 2208 BC. Since the time of the great Yu, who probably was cited as author only for the reflected luster of his name, the book has passed through numerous editions and revisions—a process that continued even beyond the era of Spanish exploration in the New World. Not all of the book's editors were even kindly disposed toward it. A few of them abridged the work severely, and for hundreds of years it was branded as little more than a compendium of folklore and superstition. Nowadays, most scholars of Chinese literature value the *Shan-hai ching* mainly as a record of early Chinese mythology.

Whatever the merits of its principal source, the theory of Chinese exploration in the New World is just one more intriguing possibility in a vast corpus of hypotheses—religious, scientific, political, and anthropological—that have been advanced to explain the origins of civilization in the Americas. And until recently, so little was understood about the distant past in this part of the world that its history was ripe for potted solutions of every description. In the last several decades, some of the mystery has begun to recede as archaeologists, historians, ethnologists, linguists, and anthropologists have accumulated a few important pieces of the puzzle. Much remains to be learned, however.

One point of general agreement is that the first Americans entered the Western Hemisphere by way of northern Asia. They came in small groups, eking out a perilous existence as hunters and gatherers of plants. The languages they spoke were widely varied, but all of them were distinct from the Indo-European tongues. Although the timing of the first migrations has never been determined conclusively, most scholars believe that the earliest settlers reached North America between 27,000 and 50,000 years ago, during the final stages of the Ice Age.

The Asian migrants traveled on foot across a now-submerged land bridge known as Beringia. Some of them pressed on farther and farther south, so that over the course of several millennia their descendants were scattered over both of the American continents. As time passed, relatively isolated pockets of population became increasingly distinct from one another. They diverged in the dialects they spoke, the religions they practiced, the social structures they adopted, and the skills they found most essential. Some tribes emphasized farming and irrigation, while others excelled in hunting, building, or metallurgy.

Beyond this generalized understanding of the ancient roots of the American peoples, relatively little is known of their history before the time of Columbus. Despite extensive archaeological exploration in all the main population centers, no well-developed sequence of cultural evolution has yet been brought to light. It is almost as though the brilliant civilizations of peoples such as the Olmec and

Toltec of Mexico and the Anasazi and Mohican to the north sprang into being untouched by the outside world. Yet there they were—building monuments worthy of the Egyptian pharaohs, designing urban public works on a par with the achievements of the civil engineers of classical Rome, and producing gold artifacts every bit the match of medieval European handicrafts. New World astronomers were no less accomplished, devising calendars that would have been the envy of Renaissance mathematicians. And the priests and the common people who spun out the Native American folklore made it every bit as rich and meaningful as the great fables of India. Modern historians and anthropologists, meanwhile, were left to ponder the source of this remarkable body of knowledge.

The scholars who grapple with this question tend to fall into two opposing camps. One group argues that human civilization could have been invented only once and that all the evidence seems to point to the conclusion that it originated somewhere in the Old World. According to this so-called diffusionist view, the pre-Columbian cultures of the Americas were largely the product of outside influences. The other group, known as isolationists, starts from precisely the opposite premise.

These historians argue that, save for some small amount of cultural baggage brought along by the Beringian migrants, all the accomplishments of the American Indian cultures were achieved independently.

In defending their theory, proponents of each view have argued the need for less than stringent standards of proof. Lacking incontrovertible physical evidence that their thesis is correct, the diffusionists rely on circumstantial evidence to validate their claims of outside cultural influences. They point to the seemingly endless list of parallel ideas and social practices that turned up in both Old and New World cultures *(page 103)*. There were, for example, nearly identical rituals for harvest celebrations among the Hebrews of the Middle East and the Yuchi Indians of the southeastern United States. Likewise, the potters of Jomon-era Japan and those of Valdivia, Chile, produced ceramics that were strikingly similar. Diffusionists are also fascinated by the similar sounds and linguistic roots that crop up in both Old and New World languages.

In calling attention to these correspondences, they hope to prove that pre-Columbian visitors to the Americas played a hand in shaping the indigenous cultures in the far distant past. Some diffusionists even suggest that the Sumerians, the Mesopotamian people credited with first devising such human advances as cities and writing, voyaged to America as early as 4,000 years ago or more. And they supposedly were followed by Egyptians, Phoenicians, Carthaginians, Israelites, Libyans, and—eventually—many European nationalities. Diffusionists also believe there were infusions of culture from across the Pacific. Intrepid explorers supposedly set out from the Indus River Valley, China, Japan, and Polynesia.

By contrast, early generations of isolationists tended to regard the oceans as all but impassable to ancient seafarers. Many isolationists now accept the possibility of Norse explorations, in about AD 1000. Some are also willing to entertain the notion that there may have been occasional contacts between shipwrecked sailors and Native American communities. But they see no convincing evidence that any of these visitors stayed long enough to exert a substantial influence. To the isolationists, then, the only way to understand Amerindian culture is to think of it as having invented itself. Scholars who adopt this perspective tend to discount the need for proof that their view is correct. They feel that logic is on their side and that, in the absence of countervailing evidence, the burden of proof should rest in the opposite camp.

Isolationists have ready answers for the long list of circumstantial evidence put forward by the diffusionists. The occasional similarities between Old and New World customs are, they believe, examples of cultural convergence. By this they mean that all people, no matter what their differences, tend to think alike. Faced with similar environmental challenges—or so the argument goes—intelligent humans are likely to react inventively in similar ways.

Thus, the fact that both Egyptians and Mayans built monumental stepped pyramids cannot be taken as an indication that the one group was influenced by the other. It would be just as logical, the isolationists assert, to infer that Mediterranean explorers must have traveled to the Arctic Circle because Eskimo igloos have structural similarities to the domes of European cathedrals. By the same token, the isolationists contend, it is not logical to assume that such practical advances as the irrigation of crops, the cultivation of cotton, spinning, weaving, papermaking, reed-boat construction, and the development of calendar systems could not have evolved independently in isolated communities.

In recent years, even scholars who dismiss the diffusionist arguments on grounds of insufficient evidence have had to concede that the oceans may not have been such formidable barriers as they once imagined. Recent historical research has shown that long before Christopher Columbus or the wide-ranging Vikings, there was a significant amount of travel on the high seas.

Among the earliest peoples to master the oceans were late-Bronze Age mariners from Mesopotamia. Perhaps as early as the third millennium BC, traders were leaving Middle Eastern ports in wooden sailing ships and sustaining a lively commerce along the length of the Mediterranean. Some of the more intrepid seafarers even ventured out beyond the Pillars of Hercules to ply their trade on the Atlantic face of the Iberian Peninsula.

More or less coincident with these voyages, the Egyptians put to sea to expand their own trade. They sent men and goods through the Red Sea to the Gulf of Aden, a 3,000-mile round trip. The first Egyptian boats were made of woven papyrus reeds, but as soon as the shipbuilders acquired cedar planks from Lebanon, they began building wooden ships as well. The papyrus vessel itself was amazingly seaworthy, as Thor Heyerdahl demonstrated in 1970, when he and seven crewmates sailed such a craft from Safin, Morocco, to the Caribbean island of Barbados. Their boat, the *Ra II*, was a forty-foot reconstruction of a single-sailed Egyp-

At the winter solstice, two daggers of sunlight stream between the standing stones (below, left) to bracket the larger (bottom left) of the two spirals carved in the cliff face. At the spring and fall equinoxes (second and fourth from left), one light shaft crosses the main spiral to the right of center, while the other, now shorter, stabs the smaller spiral through the middle. At the summer solstice (third from left), a single blade of light slices down the center of the main spiral. Remarkably, although the sun traverses the sky horizontally, the slits between slabs make the light daggers progress vertically.

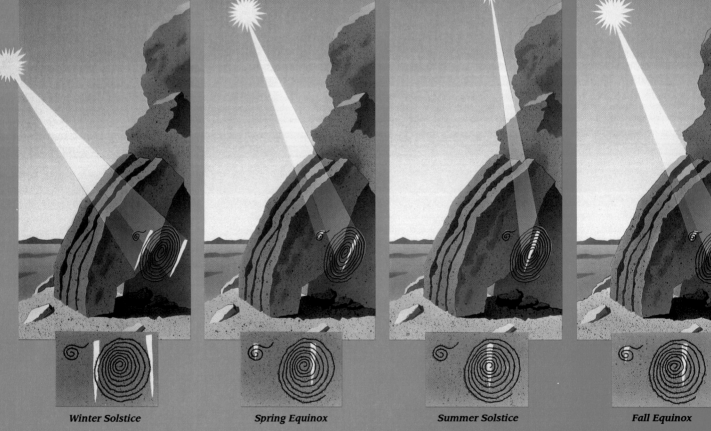

Winter Solstice   **Spring Equinox**   **Summer Solstice**   **Fall Equinox**

The Anasazi Sun Dagger nestles beneath the brow of Fajada Butte (far left), 443 feet above the floor of Chaco Canyon. The Sun Dagger's three 2-ton slabs of rock (near left) were thought by some anthropologists to have fallen into place accidentally, but geologic studies showed that they had been intentionally erected. In recent years, the middle slab has shifted, possibly from water erosion, and the Sun Dagger is no longer accurate. To prevent further damage, the site has been closed to visitors except some Native Americans who still practice a few traditional rituals involving the monument.

Dagger of the Sun

In 1977, amateur archaeologist Anna Sofaer climbed 443 treacherous feet up a butte in New Mexico's Chaco Canyon and discovered an ancient artifact of stunning importance: the Anasazi Sun Dagger. Built to mark solar time, the sophisticated stone device indicates a staggeringly high level of geometric and astronomical skill among the Anasazi people, a prehistoric culture that all but vanished eight centuries ago.

The Sun Dagger, at first glance a haphazard assemblage of rocks and spiral petroglyphs, tracked the sun's seasonal movements. For a few minutes around noon on the spring and fall equinoxes and the summer and winter solstices, sunlight shining between three slabs of sandstone fell in distinctive patterns on one or both of two carved spirals *(inset and drawings at left below)*, thus dividing the year into quarters.

In capturing beams of the midday sun as a means of timekeeping, the Anasazi Sun Dagger is unusual among ancient astronomical tools. Most other such devices, including England's great Stonehenge observatory, detect the solstices by sighting the sun's position on the horizon at sunrise.

tian reed boat, circa 1500 BC. They managed to complete a 3,270-mile voyage through sometimes dangerous seas in just fifty-seven days.

Also formidable in their nautical skills were the Phoenician mariners who colonized the land of Tarshish. This domain is mentioned in the Bible and is thought by some historians to have been located in the south of Spain. The seamen of Tarshish were greatly celebrated for their derring-do. Their merchant ships, called *gaulos* or "buckets" because of their broad-beamed hulls, averaged fifty to sixty feet in length and could transport a cargo of 50 to 100 tons along with a crew of twenty. The gaulos were comparable in size and capacity to the Portuguese caravels of the fifteenth and sixteenth centuries.

Aided only by the auxiliary power of oarsmen, the earliest Mediterranean ships were largely dependent on following winds and favorable currents to take them where they wanted to go. By the time of the Phoenician ascendancy, however, sailors were becoming proficient in the use of square-rigged sails, which gave them improved mobility when sailing into or across the wind.

The Greek historian Herodotus recorded that, as early as 600 BC, the pharaoh Necho dispatched a squadron of sailing vessels from Tarshish to explore the full length of the African coastline. Stopping periodically to replenish their stores of food and water, the mariners took nearly three years to circumnavigate the continent. If Herodotus's report was accurate, the intrepid seamen had journeyed no less than 15,000 miles.

Following the Phoenicians in the exploration of Africa was a Carthaginian adventurer named Hanno, who led a large expedition to colonize the coastal lands to the south of Gibraltar. Based on contemporary accounts, it appears that Hanno's fleet traveled perhaps 6,000 miles in all, journeying as far south as present-day Liberia. At about the same time, Hanno's countryman, Himilco, sailed north along the coast of France all the way to Brittany.

Even more remarkable was the voyage of a Greek captain, Pytheas of Massilia, who sailed north along the Atlantic coast of Europe in 300 BC, looking for sources of tin and amber. As nearly as can be ascertained from the accounts of this journey, Pytheas seems to have traveled as many as 8,000 miles through stormy seas and frigid weather. He apparently sailed through the Irish Sea to the northernmost reaches of present-day Scotland and a place he named Thule—probably the Shetland Islands. Then he struck eastward to Norway and the Baltic, before heading home via the English Channel. In the report that Pytheas later wrote, he told of summer nights that lasted only two or three hours and of a place beyond reckoning where the sun would shine at midnight over a "congealed sea"—most likely a reference to frozen waters. The wanderings of the Greek captain would define for many generations the limits of the known world.

On the other side of the globe, Polynesians were already sailing across vast reaches of the Pacific Ocean as early as 2500 BC, as they set off on their millennia-long epoch of migration that left them inhabiting islands in every part of the great ocean. With the exception of this one adventurous seagoing race, however, it appears that long-distance navigation was considerably less common in the Pacific than it was in the Atlantic.

The first significant voyages by mariners other than the Polynesians probably took place around the third century AD. The Chinese were the great power in Asia prior to that time, and their achievements were mainly confined to dry land. To the extent that the Chinese built ships at all prior to AD 200, they made mostly flat-bottomed craft, suitable for river transport, and they rarely ventured far offshore. The people of India during that era were somewhat more experienced at sea, having established a colony on Java. But historians believe that the voyages undertaken by Indian mariners were generally short jaunts along their coasts or jumps between islands. Still, there were many ancient vessels plying the edges of the Pacific, just as there were in the Atlantic. And certain historians contend that, even if the mariners of the ancient Near East or Asia never purposely attempted to cross either ocean, there had to be some whose vessels became either hopelessly lost or disabled. It is entirely possible that a few of these may have fetched up in strange lands very far from home.

Thor Heyerdahl believes that ocean currents alone might have been enough to transport sailors to the New World. He cites two such current-driven "conveyor belts" in the Atlantic and another in the Pacific. The more northerly Atlantic approach runs from Norway to Newfoundland by way of Iceland and is favored, in Heyerdahl's view, "by very short oversea distances and a fast, south-sweeping current along the east and south coasts of Greenland." A longer course, farther to the south, originates along the coast of Morocco and follows the Canaries Current to the Gulf of Mexico. This is the conveyor belt that helped propel Columbus on his journeys of exploration. A natural return route from the New World to Europe is the Gulf Stream, which originates in the Gulf of Mexico and sweeps across the North Atlantic to England.

In the Pacific, Heyerdahl cites the basically eastward-flowing Japan, or Kuroshio, Current, which runs from the Philippine Sea to the northwest coast of North America before turning south to the Isthmus of Panama. Natural conveyance in the opposite direction is provided by the North Equatorial Current and favorable trade winds. In 1947, Heyerdahl demonstrated the practicality of riding such currents when he put to sea on *Kon-Tiki (page 93).*

At one time or another, diffusionist historians have described scores of purported voyages to the New World that would have taken advantage of natural forces such as those cited by Thor Heyerdahl. Of all the alleged visits, two stand

Braving the North Atlantic in a thirty-six-foot replica of a medieval boat, British sailor Timothy Severin (inset) and his crew re-create in 1977 a legendary voyage. Attempting to duplicate Saint Brendan's fabled route, they sailed 2,600 miles from Ireland to Newfoundland.

out as the most probable or believable: the Viking explorations, already mentioned, and a possible sojourn by Irish missionaries during the sixth century AD. The likelihood of an Irish visit is still a point of controversy. If the stories are true, however, the voyages would have predated a Viking contact by several centuries.

The notion of Irishmen visiting pre-Columbian America came from legends concerning Saint Brendan, also known as Brendan the Navigator. The tales first circulated early in the sixth century and were well known across Europe some 200 years later. Their appealing hero was born in County Kerry in the closing decades of the fifth century, not long after Saint Patrick brought Christianity to Ireland. Brendan apparently joined the clergy in his youth and rose by dint of personal magnetism and moral strength to be a leading figure in Irish church affairs. He was personally responsible for establishing monasteries in Kerry and Galway and traveled widely to other religious centers in Scotland, Wales, England, and France.

At some point in his long, full life, which was said to span more than nine decades, Brendan set off on a quest for self-knowledge. In doing so, he helped establish a tradition among Irish monks. The monks made a point of removing themselves from human contact—often by sailing to some offshore speck of land—and giving themselves over to solitude and contemplation, sometimes for years at a time. The rock-rimmed islands that these monk-mariners sought out were the Irish equivalent of the desert hideaways favored by the Christian anchorites of North Africa. The specific circumstances of

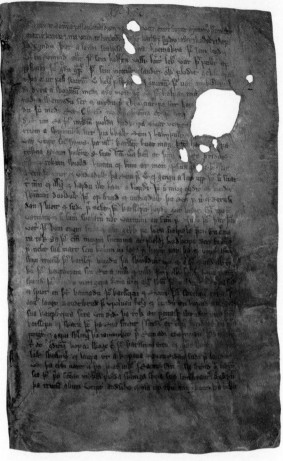

A page from the old Viking epic known as Eric's Saga tells how—five centuries before Columbus—Norse colonists in America traded and warred with the "wretches" who lived there.

Brendan's adventure can be pieced together only from various partial accounts of his life. The *Navigatio Sancti Brendani,* a tenth-century manuscript of unknown authorship, relates that while the Irish cleric was planning his voyage, an aged colleague, Abbot Barinth, told him of a voyage of his own. Barinth claimed to have stumbled on the fabled *terra repromissionis sanctorum,* the Promised Land of Saints. He described it as being every bit as wonderful as one might imagine, a kind of earthly paradise. To prove his point, the abbot urged Brendan to sniff his cloak, which had somehow retained the fragrance of flowers that it had taken on during his sojourn in the magical place. Captivated by the abbot's story, Brendan gathered fourteen companions and set to work building a boat.

The author of the *Navigatio* described the craft as "a very light little vessel, ribbed and sided with wood, but . . . covered with oak-tanned oxhides and caulked with ox-tallow." Historians recognize this as a description of the Irish currach, a versatile, spacious, nearly round boat, which was open to the elements but capable of bobbing atop the waves like a watertight wicker basket.

When the currach was fully rigged, Brendan and his crew loaded aboard water, wine, and victuals for forty days and set off to the west with Almighty God as their pilot. According to the *Life of St. Brendan,* another rather poetic telling of the Irishman's saga, the band of monks sailed for years "over the loud-voiced waves of the rough-crested sea, and over the billows of the greenish tide, and over the abysses of the wonderful, terrible, relentless ocean." In the course of their voyage, they encountered many marvelous things, including sea monsters, avian choirs, saints, and devils, as well as a whale that they briefly mistook for an island, until it sank beneath their feet. Their patience and fortitude were eventually rewarded when they came to the promised land, which struck them as a blessed place. After exploring the interior for forty days, during which time Brendan received a prophecy of his own death, they set sail for home to recount their remarkable story.

For all the fanciful embellishments, most modern historians regard the legend of Saint Brendan as containing at least some kernel of the truth. Many scholars assume that the exaggeratedly long duration of the voyage must be regarded as a tip-off that the story is a composite of many different voyages by Irish sailors over a century or more. They suspect that even the figure of Saint Brendan is more than likely a pastiche of various heroes.

One reason Brendan's story is given credence is that later Viking historians corroborated the notion of Irish monks having preceded them to their far-flung destinations. This has to be regarded as generous credit, coming from an exploring people, and the Vikings probably would not have extended it lightly. Moreover, archaeologists have found physical evidence of a long-ago Irish presence in places such as the Faeroe Islands and Iceland. Unfortunately, there seems to be no way of ascertaining the identity of the Promised Land of Saints, or the Isle of Saint Brendan, as medieval chroniclers came to call it. Mapmakers of later centuries always portrayed this land on the perimeters of the known world, usually to the west or among the Canaries and the Azores. Lacking hard information about the place, they gave it many shapes and sizes. The degree to which early cartographers were willing to document purely speculative geographical information may be judged by a Portuguese manual on ocean navigation that was written in 1514; it contained one entire chapter filled with instructions on how to sail to "islands not yet discovered."

Despite the difficulties posed by such free-form scholarship, historian Geoffrey Ashe believes that it is possible to trace at least some of Brendan's voyage on the basis of the *Navigatio*. After studying the book's detailed accounts of the distances the monks claimed to have traveled and the time they supposedly spent at sea, he came to believe that the story had "every appearance of being based upon competent research. . . . It portrays a land of continental size a long way off across the Atlantic, behind a curtain of fog at about the correct distance from the Faeroes." Ashe is also impressed by the *Navigatio's* apt descriptions of places such as the Bahamas and Jamaica. He is not ready to state that Brendan himself actually made the journey, but he believes that someone must have done so in order to write such a knowing chronicle. Ashe credits Saint Brendan and others like him with having set the minds of their contemporaries toward exploring new worlds. Indeed, five centuries later, Columbus acknowledged his debt to the venturesome monk when he swore to reveal, once and for all, the truth about Brendan's "earthly paradise" to the west.

Certainly, the exploits of the Irish monks were familiar—at least in a general way—to the Norsemen who set sail westward. And it is entirely possible that some of what the Irish learned at sea may have contributed to the success of the Vikings in finding their way to the new lands. The evidence relating to the Norse excursions includes the many references to Western exploration in the sagas of the Vikings. There are also numerous artifacts and other archaeological indications of temporary settlements that have been linked to the Norse visits. The main questions that linger about the Norse expeditions have to do with when the explorers first set foot in North America, how deep into the interior they traveled, and the degree to which they may have influenced the indigenous peoples.

The sagas were passed along verbally for many gener-

ations before they were written down for the first time at the start of the thirteenth century. They indicate that the Vikings made several westward forays, beginning perhaps as early as AD 800. At about that time, the first of the Norse explorers were settling on the fog-shrouded Shetland, Faeroe, and Orkney islands to the north and the west of Scotland. Later expeditions are better documented, especially those recounted in the *Groenlendina,* or *Greenlanders' Saga,* and retold with some alterations in the chronicle known as *Eric's Saga.*

According to these works, a man named Erik the Red was expelled from the Norse community in Iceland in the year 982, following a violent dispute in which two of his neighbors were slain. Banished from the island for three years, he sailed off in search of a new home. Having heard tales of an earlier explorer named Gunnbjorn, who had sighted land to the west of Iceland, Erik set sail in that direction. He was well equipped for the voyage in his seaworthy wooden *knarr,* and he had the good fortune to come upon what he took to be a huge peninsula. Eric called his discovery Greenland.

After reconnoitering the southern coast of the place for a considerable time, he put ashore at a site just to the west of what is now known as Cape Farewell. There, he waited out his three-year exile, then returned to Iceland to recruit other settlers for his new community. Soon Greenland had several small colonies along its shores.

Not long after Erik had returned to his village, his second son, Leif, grew restless. According to the *Greenlanders' Saga,* "there was now great talk of discovering new countries" among more adventurous Norsemen. This was thanks in part to the chance sighting of several wooded islands by another mariner, Bjarni Herjolfsson. Bjarni had lost his way at sea and, in his haste to recover his bearings, had chosen not to investigate the islands he had spied. Given the prevailing attitudes of the time, it is perhaps significant that Bjarni was treated with mild contempt in the saga on account of his caution and lack of curiosity. In any event, Leif resolved to retrace Bjarni's course and put to sea with a crew of thirty-five men in about the year 1000. He island-hopped to the west, stopping only briefly at an inhospitable place he named Slab Land and lingering more appreciatively at a spot he called Forest Land, where he admired the white, sandy beaches. Eventually, Leif fetched up at a locale so delightful in setting, vegetation, and climate that he named it Vinland the Good—a place that was, evidently, as pleasing as wine.

According to the sagas, Leif decided to winter in Vinland, so he and his men rowed their knarr some distance up a river estuary. They came at last to a quiet anchorage on the shores of a lake and carried their belongings ashore. Leif returned to Greenland the following year, but others, including the explorer's brother Thorvald, made the journey to Vinland. They probably would have established a permanent settlement had it not been for hostile natives, whom the Norsemen referred to as Skraelings. A deadly clash with Skraelings made the newcomers long for the relative safety of Iceland and Greenland.

Through most of the nineteenth century, scholars looked upon the accounts of Leif Eriksson's odyssey as little more than fairy tales. The sagas that described the Viking explorations were written in the style of heroic literature, contrived to entertain and elicit pride of race. It was natural, therefore, to take them with a grain of salt. The few historians who bothered to read these chronicles with an eye to their historical content faced problems at every turn. For one thing, different versions of the stories seemed to flatly contradict one another. It was nearly impossible to resolve the conflicting reports on practical details such as sailing distances and times. And from the standpoint of serious scholarship, it was hard to ignore the Viking's milk-and-honey descriptions of the lands that they found. These were, after all, places that were quite severe in climate and stark in their natural landscapes. Passages such as one that described a North Atlantic island as having weather so gentle that "no winter fodder would be needed for livestock" gave the sagas the texture of fiction.

By the beginning of the twentieth century, however, evidence was accumulating that the essential story of Vinland was almost certainly true. Ironically, some of the evidence that began to turn the tide of scholarly opinion would later prove to be fraudulent. For the time being, though, the biggest problem lay in figuring out where Vinland was. A literal reading of the Norse chronicles seemed to suggest Newfoundland as a likely candidate, but references to birch trees, grapes, and wild wheat pointed to a habitat farther to the south, one with a somewhat more temperate climate. The mouth of the St. Lawrence River was considered a possibility, as were Nova Scotia, Maine, Cape Cod, Rhode Island, New Jersey, and even Virginia. Some scholars speculated that Leif may not have stopped at his first landfall but may have wended his way through inland waterways deep into the interior of his newly discovered continent.

In the 1960s, Norwegian explorer and writer Helge Ingstad undertook to unravel the mystery. He was convinced that the *Greenlanders' Saga* was more than just a fable and that by taking seriously its accounts of Leif Eriksson's travels he might locate the explorer's winter camp. Working on a hunch that the *vin* in *Vinland* referred not to grapes but to an old Norse word meaning "grazing land," he decided to search in Newfoundland first.

After fruitless hunting in many ports, Ingstad found himself one day in a tiny northern village called L'Anse aux Meadows. He made his usual inquiries about old ruins or other signs of early habitation, and he was lucky enough to meet a villager who recalled hearing about some curious rock formations in fields not far from the village. The man escorted Ingstad to the place, which struck the writer as exceedingly pleasant pastureland for such a northerly location. It was, in his words, "an inviting place, peaceful and untouched." Hiking farther inland along the bed of a stream, he came to a small lake, much like the one described in the saga of Leif's winter anchorage. Ingstad saw, too, a number of soddy "bumps" in the otherwise flattish land and the ruins of three very old cairns. As he gazed toward the sea, he became more and more convinced that the landscapes surrounding him were the ones extolled in the old Norse stories.

Ingstad returned the following summer with his wife, Anne Stine Ingstad, who is a professional archaeologist, and a crew of four helpers. They set to work digging and, in a short time, unearthed a slate-lined firepit that was strik-

ingly similar to the old Viking hearths found in Greenland. Greatly encouraged, the couple planned extensive excavations and, over the course of several digging seasons, uncovered evidence of a substantial settlement.

Just below the sod that covered the site, the Ingstads found the outlines of a Norse "great house" measuring

The Odd Tale of a Lost Welsh Colony

As white settlers headed west across America, they heard strange tales of tribes of "white" Indians who spoke a language said to be much like Welsh and who followed some European religious customs. Frontier travelers—including the legendary Daniel Boone—told of seeing these blue-eyed, fair-skinned natives in places ranging from British Columbia to Peru and from the Dakotas to Florida.

The white Indians were variously explained as descendants of the ten lost tribes of Israel, the legacy of a Portuguese shipwreck, the result of desertions in Hernando de Soto's forces, and the remnants of Sir Walter Raleigh's Lost Colony of Roanoke Island on the Atlantic. One of the most prevalent explanations, however, concerned a Welsh prince named Madoc.

Said to be a son of a Welsh ruler, Madoc supposedly led an expedition in AD 1170 to explore the western reaches of the Atlantic. Among his alleged anchorages was the site now known as Mobile Bay, Alabama. Supporters of the "Welsh Indian" theory said these explorers made their way inland, intermarried, and passed on their language, customs, and genetic characteristics. In time, their offspring may have migrated as far north as the Dakotas.

Nineteenth-century painter and frontiersman George Catlin was convinced that the Mandan tribe of the Dakotas

were descendants of Madoc. He described the Mandans as "friendly and hospitable" and became quite attached to Chief Mah-to-toh-pa, whose portrait he painted *(left)*. "At the moment that I first saw these people," he wrote, "I was so struck with the peculiarity of their appearance, that I was under the instant conviction that they were an amalgam of a native with some civilised race."

Among the evidence presented by Catlin was the Welsh word *Mandon*, which referred to a plant used to make red dye. The Mandan Indians, said Catlin, worked with beautiful red dyes in staining the porcupine quills that were part of their costumery. He also suggested that the tribe's name may have been a corruption of the Welsh word *Madawgwys*, (followers of Madawc). The Mandan canoes, Catlin also claimed, were "altogether different from those of all other tribes," and more like the tublike Welsh coracle.

Whether the Mandans were descended from the Welsh may never be proved. The tribe was almost totally destroyed by smallpox. The theory persists, however, and in 1953, at Fort Morgan, Alabama, a memorial tablet was dedicated. It reads, "In memory of Prince Madoc, a Welsh explorer, who landed on the shores of Mobile Bay in 1170 and left behind, with the Indians, the Welsh Language."

eighty by eighteen feet. They also saw signs of two smaller halls and several other modest dwellings and boathouses. Uncovering these ruins was exciting, but what the Ingstads really needed were artifacts that would clearly link the settlement to the Norse explorers. In 1962, they began to set hands on such items. They first unearthed a tool used for honing needles that was similar to those used by Viking women. This was followed by a piece of smelted copper, some iron slag, a ring-headed bronze pin, and a few bits of charcoal that were shown by radiocarbon dating to have been produced sometime between the ninth and eleventh centuries. These latter finds were of particular significance, because historians had already established that the native inhabitants of Newfoundland did not master the smelting process until several centuries later.

The discoveries at L'Anse aux Meadows were the first commonly accepted archaeological proofs of European presence in the Americas before the time of Columbus. They showed that, at the very least, the Norse people had reached the Western Hemisphere as early as the eleventh century and had stayed long enough to establish a colony, which included women and children. The Ingstads could not, however, confirm beyond a reasonable doubt that the ruins at L'Anse aux Meadows had belonged to Leif Eriksson or that Newfoundland was indeed the Vinland of the Norse sagas. Nor was it their purpose to examine the ways in which the Viking settlers may have exerted an influence on the indigenous cultures in the new land. Nevertheless, the excavations carried out by Helge and Anne Ingstad were of great historical significance.

Of distinctly different pedigree are the dozens of alleged Viking artifacts that have turned up in places as far to the south and to the west of Newfoundland as Oklahoma and the Great Lakes.

Although such finds have sustained several generations of amateur historians, who would love to believe that the Norse explorers traveled widely in the New World, few of the discoveries have won many converts within the ar-

chaeological establishment. A few, in fact, proved to be downright embarrassing.

Perhaps the most troublesome of the artifacts was the so-called Kensington Stone, which came to light in 1898. This slab weighing nearly 200 pounds was unearthed in the farming village of Kensington, Minnesota, by a farmer named Olof Ohman. It is covered with runic inscriptions that are suggestive of medieval Scandinavian writing and tell of a Swedish-Norwegian expedition in 1362, several generations after Leif Eriksson's voyage to Vinland. According to reports published at the time, Ohman found the stone tangled in the roots of a poplar tree, which he had cut down while clearing a pasture.

Ohman's discovery came at a time of heightened interest in the Vinland voyages. In 1892, a convention in Chicago had attracted a good deal of attention by including an exhibit on the Vikings and a replica of one of their ocean-going vessels. When stories about Ohman's peculiar stone tablet began appearing in newspapers across the country, specialists in the translation of rune inscriptions were eager to take a look. To the disappointment of the large Scandinavian-American population living in and around Kensington, the scholars were unanimous in declaring the stone a hoax. For his part, Ohman was so upset that he stashed the stone in his barn and went back to work, hoping the whole matter would blow over.

In 1907, however, another Scandinavian-American, Hjalmar R. Holand, was writing a history of Norse immigration to the New World and purchased the stone from Ohman. He launched a campaign to reevaluate the significance of his acquisition and to take a fresh look at the impact of the Norse explorations in the Americas. In the years that followed, Holand churned out three volumes of theorizing on the wandering of the ancient Norsemen—and on the special significance of what came to be called the Kensington Stone. Among his other rather dubious contributions, Holand may be responsible for the erroneous belief that certain holes found in rocks along the shores of Lake Superior were made by the Norsemen for the purpose of

Ancient Native American petroglyphs crowd the twelve-foot-high face of a boulder at Rochester Creek, Utah. According to some researchers, these drawings not only resemble certain Egyptian hieroglyphics (inset), they depict Egyptian myth. As interpreted by British Egyptologist Gwyn Griffiths, the soul (1) climbing a rope ladder toward heaven is threatened by a hippopotamus—never seen near Utah—and defended by the jackal god Anubis and a man with a stick (2). Owls (3) and serpents (4 and 5) were prominent in Egyptian religious myth.

securing their boats for the night. Subsequent research has shown that the holes were not nearly as old as the Vikings; they were made by surveyors marking the land and by engineers engaged in blasting with dynamite.

In the early decades of the twentieth century, however, Holand's pronouncements captured the imagination of Viking enthusiasts, who numbered in the thousands. And as late as 1949, M. W. Stirling, director of the Smithsonian Institution's American Bureau of Ethnology, was attesting to the authenticity of the Kensington Stone, which he called "probably the most important archaeological object yet found in North America." Although the relic has since come under heavy attack, many diffusionist historians continue to hold similar views.

Thoroughly unimpressed by the arguments of the Kensington Stone's supporters, the overwhelming majority of mainstream historians regard it as nothing more than an amusing forgery. Linguistic specialists point out that the text of the runic inscription is not in keeping with writing styles of the fourteenth century—the time in which it would have been created. Other examiners have noted that the inscriptions have not weathered in a way that would indicate great age and that the characters have every appearance of having been produced with modern, steel-edged chisels. No one knows enough to allege with certainty that farmer Olof Ohman actually collaborated in forging the inscription. The other distinct possibility is that the Kensington Stone was simply deposited on Ohman's property with the expectation that it would be discovered sooner or later.

There is also no proof that promoters such as Hjalmar Holand knew the stone was a hoax. Holand may have simply been an opportunist, or even a perfectly sincere believer in the stone. What is clear is that he parlayed his interest in the artifact into a lifelong career. Of course, he was not alone in recognizing a good thing when he saw it: Even the nearby town of Alexandria, Minnesota, got into the act, seeking funding for a state park, then bestowing on itself the dubious title "Birthplace of America."

While the Kensington Stone controversy was playing itself out, other supposed artifacts turned up from time to time, and they generally included puzzling runic inscriptions. The most publicized discovery of recent years was a group of three inscribed stones that were found near Popham Beach, Maine, in 1971. Depending on whom you speak to, these so-called Spirit Pond rune-stones are either the work of prankish college students or a terribly significant archaeological find.

The Spirit Pond artifacts turned up on the shore of a saltwater inlet, where an amateur treasure hunter and beachcomber stumbled over them. They are all less than a foot across and contain several generally incoherent messages and a smattering of cartoonlike pictographs. One of the stones bears a peculiar map. Perhaps the most generous assessment of the discovery came from Cyrus Gordon, who headed the Department of Mediterranean Studies at Brandeis University for thirteen years during the 1960s and 1970s. In Gordon's view, the inscriptions on the stones were "plaintext gibberish," but their very obscurity only served to prove their genuineness. They were a "labyrinth of ingenuity," Gordon asserted, and typical of the work of ancient rune makers. He believed that it was a mistake to expect runic inscriptions to conform to any standards of idiomatic speech or spelling. "Many a medieval runemaster," Gordon wrote, "felt that such simple expression was for simpletons, not for the educated elite." By implication, his elitist rune makers would have wanted to communicate with only a chosen few.

Gordon and a few like-thinking contemporaries believe that the Spirit Pond Stones can be comprehended only through a complicated decoding process. Hidden messages, they believe, are conveyed in vertical columns, using the first and last letters of each line of text. Reading the markings in this way—and granting themselves a fair amount of latitude for interpretation—Gordon and his confreres have come to the conclusion that the Spirit Pond Stones recount the spiritual mission of a long-ago bishop of Greenland, named Henricus, who like many of his countrymen journeyed to the New World.

Few mainstream historians are at all tolerant of this notion. Typical of those who reject Gordon's thesis is historian Erik Wahlgren, who published a study called *The Vikings and America* in 1986. Wahlgren devotes a chapter of his work to deflating what he considers to be a century or so of unadulterated "Norsemania." He takes particular aim at the Spirit Pond rune-stones, which he considers an amusing hoax. Among the other shortcomings in the inscription that Wahlgren points out is a reference to the territory of Canada, which was not a national entity until almost nine centuries after the year 1011, when the stone was allegedly inscribed. He suspects that a more accurate date for the inscription is probably closer to 1970.

Rune-stones were not the only artifacts to capture the imagination of Vikingologists and the scorn of academicians. According to Geoffrey Ashe, two flared axes, one from Nova Scotia, the other from Cape Cod, enjoyed a brief celebrity but were later revealed to be of nineteenth-century manufacture. A second group of Viking halberds caused considerable excitement when they were unearthed in the Midwest. Before long, however, some scholarly spoilsport showed that the would-be weapons were actually tools for cutting plug tobacco. They were made for the American Tobacco Company to be used as premiums and promotional displays for a product called Battle Axe Tobacco. And in another peculiar episode, a Canadian

Neil M. Judd, Smithsonian Institution curator of archaeology, examines runes on the controversial Kensington Stone under a magnifier in 1948. The Smithsonian exhibited the stone, which many consider proof that Scandinavians reached America before Columbus. Later the stone was moved to Alexandria, Minnesota's Runestone Museum.

cache that included a Viking-style sword, an ax head, and a fragment of a very old rattle from a horse's bridle proved to be authentic, but the story of their 1923 discovery in Beardmore, Ontario, turned out to be a ruse. All of the artifacts had been part of a private collection in Europe, until the publicity-minded son of the original collector sought to enhance their value by having them rediscovered.

In a category all by itself is the case of the so-called Vinland Map, which had the distinction of catching some rather prominent academic fish in its fraudulent net. At least some of the scholars who were taken in by this discovery really should have known better. The Vinland Map was purportedly a fifteenth-century chart of the Atlantic Ocean that actually identified Leif Eriksson's great discovery, as well as several other islands that he visited.

The parchment map came to light in 1957, when a New Haven antiquary purchased an old manuscript into which the chart had been bound. The collector paid $3,500 for his find in Barcelona, then skimmed a tidy profit when he turned around and sold the map to Yale University for a sum reputed to be more than $250,000. After five years of presumably exhaustive study by various scholars at Yale and the British Museum, a facsimile of the map and a raft of supporting documents were published with great fanfare. The map, Yale declared, settled once and for all the question of Vinland's existence and proved that Leif Eriksson had preceded Columbus to the Americas.

Serious doubts were soon raised, however, and not only by Columbus-proud Italians who might resent the implications of the map. Cartographic historians, in particular, found much to wonder about in the document, including its astonishing accuracy for a work of its era. Yale University decided that it could put to rest such concerns only by submitting the treasure to spectrographic analysis. Much to the school's embarrassment, the independent testers discovered that some of the inks used in drawing the map contained infinitesimal amounts of anatase. This is a form of titanium dioxide that has been used as a pigment since the 1920s, when it was first manufactured.

A few dogged defenders of the map suggested that the inauthentic inks may have been part of a clumsy attempt at restoration and that the document was otherwise genuine. After further studies, however, it was revealed that the anatase was simply too pervasive for the map to be anything but a forgery. Eventually, scholars ferreted out the true story: The Vinland Map had been drawn in 1922, shortly before the death of its creator, a Yugoslavian priest and professor named Luka Jelic. The cleric's motives in passing off this fake have never been established, but it is known that he nurtured a longstanding grudge about his lack of prestige at the Catholic seminary where he taught. There is also speculation that the priest was hoping to achieve a sort of immortality through his duplicity—and who is to say that he failed to achieve that goal.

In addition to artifacts such as maps, battle-axes, and inscribed stones, there are two freestanding structures in North America that are frequently cited as evidence of Viking colonization. One that has long been a well-known landmark is a small stone tower in Newport, Rhode Island. This edifice was already a fixture of the Newport cityscape in 1677, when it was first mentioned in local historical records. But the tower had fallen into disrepair and was largely ignored until 1839, when a Danish antiquary, Carl Rafn, suggested that it was the remains of an ancient Norse baptistery. According to Rafn, the tower had stood on the same spot since the eleventh or twelfth century.

Newporters rallied around this idea—perhaps sensing the value of another local tourist attraction. Henry Wadsworth Longfellow was smitten by the theory and composed a ballad called "The Skeleton in Armor," which celebrated the possibility of an epoch of Norse culture in the region. Fellow Bostonian James Russell Lowell thought the whole idea was ridiculous, however, and made no secret of his scorn. He wrote a satire in which he elucidated the three types of clues bequeathed by the passing centuries: There were those understandable to the Danish Royal Society of Northern Antiquaries, those that only scholar Rafn could appreciate, and those that were totally unintelligible to the whole of humankind. Evidence that fit in the final category, he declared, was generally deemed the most valuable.

Not until 1948 did anyone bother to look seriously for archaeological clues that might support or refute Rafn's claim. That year William Godfrey, Jr., of Massachusetts's Peabody Museum conducted excavations on the grounds around the tower. From the standpoint of the Newport chamber of commerce, the results were not good. Godfrey found nothing older than Colonial-era pottery and was forced to conclude that the mysterious building had probably been either a lookout tower or a windmill. He estimated that the time of its construction was approximately 1640. This still made the tower one of the oldest structures in America—a noteworthy distinction—but it was a severe disappointment to the Vikingologists.

Another old structure that has been linked with the Norse explorers is the so-called Mystery Hill complex in North Salem, New Hampshire. This is a cluster of twenty-two cellarlike chambers. The structures are unusual in their design: Some of them have huge rock slabs as their roofs and similarly large stones for doorposts and vertical supports, rather like Stonehenge in England. Some of the cellars were built above ground and then covered over with mounded earth. Originally known as Pattee's Caves, in honor of the nineteenth-century Yankee farmer on whose property they were located, Mystery Hill has been a curiosity for more than a century. During that time, various diffusionist historians have attributed the construction of the cellars to Norse, Irish, and even Phoenician explorers.

In 1955, Junius Bird of the American Museum of Natural History directed an early scientific excavation of Mystery Hill. More than 7,000 artifacts were retrieved, and all but a handful were found to date from the Colonial period or later. The exceptions were of American Indian manufacture—a few of them very old indeed. Bird and his associates concluded that the structures were either Colonial root cellars or some sort of hiding place, possibly for use in a bootleg-whiskey operation.

By the time of Bird's investigation, however, the Mystery Hill property had passed into the hands of a man named Robert Stone, who was not persuaded by the scientific findings. Stone believed that the site was far older than the era of British colonialism in America or even of the Norse explorations. He was convinced that it dated from prehistoric times, and he joined forces with a number of other amateur historians who were intrigued by other old stone chambers scattered throughout New England. Stone and his cohorts formed the New England Antiquities Research Association and proceeded to catalog more than a hundred presumedly ancient stoneworks in the Northeast. In time, their work attracted the attention of a scholar at Harvard named Barry Fell.

At the time, Fell was employed as a specialist in invertebrate zoology and was little more than a hobbyist when it came to history. But he had a deep-seated interest in ancient cultures and had followed the work of a number of diffusionist theorists. Eventually, he would share Stone's belief in the antiquity of Mystery Hill and would write about the New Hampshire ruins in the context of an elaborate personal vision of pre-Columbian America.

Raised in New Zealand, Fell had come to his fascination with history by way of an earlier interest in languages. As a young man, he had taught himself to speak Maori, the dialect of the indigenous people of New Zealand. Later he mastered the Celtic tongue, which he studied while completing his doctorate in zoology. After becoming familiar with several other ancient languages—Sanskrit among them—Fell began to perceive what he considered to be connections among languages that have always been regarded as totally unrelated. He saw parallels, for example, between North African dialects and the speech patterns of the Nordic peoples. These observations led him to a broader consideration of the historical trends that might have brought about surprising linguistic linkages. Fell began spending his summers traveling in North America and Europe and studying the ancient inscriptions he found at archaeological sites.

By the time he visited Mystery Hill, he was writing the

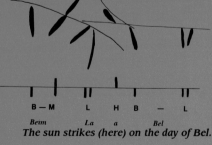

B — M   L   H   B   —   L

Beim   *La*   *a*   *Bel*

The sun strikes (here) on the day of Bel.

Calling Cards of Ancient Visitors

Carved into cliffs, caves, and rocks, inscriptions called oghams—such as those shown at left—may prove that the New World hummed with European travelers for centuries before Columbus sailed. Undeciphered until the late 1970s, such messages were scattered across North America; these were found in Vermont *(top),* West Virginia *(middle),* and Colorado *(bottom photograph and drawing).*

Oghams are named for the ancient alphabet in which they are said to be written. The characters are groups of straight or slanted strokes, crossing or touching a center line—which may be left uncarved, only implied. First used in a book in twelfth-century Ireland, ogham letters were carved on Celtic tombstones for centuries before that.

In the controversial view of some authorities, such as Harvard scholar Barry Fell, an earlier, vowel-free form of ogham was used to write the American inscriptions as early as 800 BC. Primarily scratched in sandstone, the markings are dismissed by some specialists as prehistoric tool-sharpening scars. Fell and others, however, have produced translations of many, including the one at left.

As translated by the epigraphists, some American oghams have religious import, some astronomical. The Colorado inscription is indeed struck by sunlight at dawn on the equinoxes. If the translation is correct, such a message would reveal the ancient presence of Europeans in North America.

first of several books setting forth his views on transoceanic exploration and commerce. As it turned out, his impressions of the ruins on Robert Stone's property helped crystallize his basic theories on history. They also persuaded him to abandon his calling as a biologist. In 1976, the part-time epigraphist published a book called *America B.C., Ancient Settlers in the New World.* According to the scenario mapped out in this work, waves of pioneers began arriving in North America around 3400 BC, when the first Iberian Celts drifted to the New World entirely by accident. When they found their way back to their homelands, they carried tales of the wonders that lay in the Americas, and their stories took root in several ancient mythologies. As mariners became more daring, Fell asserted, deliberate Atlantic crossings were undertaken, beginning in about 1000 BC.

Fell's list of post-Iberian visitors is extraordinarily varied: It includes Phoenician traders, who did business, he said, with the Wabanaki Indians of New England, and mariners from Libya and Egypt, who purportedly sailed up the Mississippi and westward along the Arkansas River to establish a colony in Iowa. Fell also had Norse and Basque visitors reaching the Gulf of St. Lawrence and leaving traces of their language in the speech of the northern Algonquin. Semitic merchants, meanwhile, were supposedly roaming the western reaches of North America and seeding the Pima Indian folklore with their distinctive story of creation. In addition, Fell contends, the Carthaginians left petroglyphs in Colorado, and a whole cross section of travelers from around the Mediterranean left inscriptions throughout the new lands. The area around one small farming town—Heavener, Oklahoma—is so laden with carved messages, Fell asserts, that it is "one of the major centers of research in ancient American epigraphy."

According to Barry Fell, the Mystery Hill complex was originally built by the Celts as an astronomical observatory. In time, the Celts saw fit to share the place with the far-ranging mariners of Phoenicia. One particular cellar, Fell believes, was used as a sort of astronomical instrument to mark the passing of the winter solstice. Inscriptions discov-

ered on the premises allegedly make reference to studies of the sun. Other inscriptions extol the sun god, Bel, in the ogham notation of the Celts, and call upon Baal, the god of the Phoenicians, in characters of the Punic alphabet. Judging by these ancient writings, Fell estimates that the age of Pattee's Caves is somewhere in the vicinity of 2,600 to 2,800 years. He is also convinced that descendants of the original settlers occupied the area for so many centuries that they were still there in residence during the first century BC, when Julius Caesar ruled Rome.

When *America B.C.* was first published in the United States, it received a great deal of attention in the popular press. Some of the publicity stemmed, no doubt, from the author's affiliation with a prestigious university (although a few of Fell's critics pointed out that he had earned his credentials in an entirely different field of research). Predictably, the reception given his thesis in the halls of academia was exceedingly cool. Historians noted that Fell had relied almost entirely on linguistic analysis of old inscriptions to support his case for multiple transoceanic contacts. And those critics who understood the languages in question challenged Fell's analysis as flawed. The consensus was that Fell had based his conclusions on highly selective bits of evidence, while studiously ignoring the great body of information that argued against his premise.

If Barry Fell was stung by the slings and arrows sent his way by colleagues in American universities, he gave no clear indication. If anything, he seemed stimulated by the controversy he had provoked and went on to publish two additional books on the subject of transoceanic travel and commerce. In the second of these volumes, *Bronze Age America,* Fell introduces a new personality to the roster of alleged New World explorers. He tells the story of King Woden-lithi, a Norse monarch who supposedly forged a trade relationship with certain Indian tribes of North America around 1700 BC.

Fell's interest in Woden-lithi began to take shape in 1976, when he studied a series of previously undeciphered rock inscriptions in Peterborough, Ontario. The epigraphs had baffled the anthropologists who had originally discovered them, being totally unlike the Algonquin art they had come to the region to study. But Fell claimed to recognize the writings as an archaic form of Scandinavian script, dating from the Bronze Age, and he determined that they recounted the voyage of a previously unknown Nordic king. According to Fell's interpretation, Woden-lithi had sailed across the Atlantic and up the St. Lawrence River in hopes of establishing trade with the Algonquin. He had brought along a cargo of woven goods, which he planned to exchange for the copper ingots that the natives possessed in abundance. Arriving in the spring, he pursued this commerce for five months before heading downriver and homeward. When he departed, the king left behind a contingent of his countrymen to keep the trading post in operation. According to Fell, the Peterborough inscriptions not only record the visit of Woden-lithi but provide an orderly accounting of his business transactions. They even include such mundane information as a standard of measure for cloth and cordage.

Woden-lithi's discoverer does not purport to know what ultimately became of the Norse colonists—whether they intermarried with the native population or simply died out. But Fell believes that, even if this particular trading mission failed to survive, the combined activities of traders from many parts of Europe probably resulted in the shipment of many tons of copper ingots over the course of several centuries. He cites as evidence what he claims are the remains of some 5,000 ancient copper mines around the northern shore of Lake Superior and the paucity of copper artifacts associated with Native Americans. If all that copper did not find a market among the Indians, he reasons, it must have been shipped overseas.

Although Barry Fell's rewriting of North American history has attracted its share of critics, he also has won many supporters, mostly from outside the field of archaeology. His work has assumed, by his own description, the character of a ministry. "It is plain that the word we bring," he wrote, "is something that many young people have longed to hear, namely that America is part of the great Western World whose roots lie in the Mediterranean and whose branches lie in far-flung continents." Fell predicts that as the focus of his work shifts to the Pacific seaboard, he will discover Oriental influences that are every bit as pervasive as those that arrived from across the Atlantic. He expects to perceive, eventually, a "synthesis of West and East that arose in the Americas."

One historian who might be considered to be part of Fell's ministry or at least to share the same "faith" is Joseph Mahan of Columbus, Georgia. In 1967, Mahan found himself at the center of an intriguing discovery that gave credence—at least in some circles—to the theory of ancient Mediterranean colonization in the New World.

The lucky strike that changed the course of Mahan's work came about one day when Manfred Metcalf, a civilian employee at Fort Benning, Georgia, was poking around the collapsed foundation of an abandoned nineteenth-century house. Metcalf was gathering stones for a backyard barbecue pit, when he picked up a flat-faced rectangle of sandstone that measured about nine inches square. Brushing off the stone, he examined it and noticed what appeared to be pictographs—a sequence of triangles, circles, and straight and wavy lines. Curious about these markings, he took the stone to the nearby city of Columbus, where he showed it to Mahan, who was the resident archaeologist at the Museum of Arts and Crafts.

An expert in Native American ethnology, Mahan had for some time been investigating the history of the Yuchi Indians, who claimed to trace their beginnings as a tribe to a greater worldwide civilization. "We came as the sun came, and we went as the sun went," a tribal elder had once said to Mahan, referring to the Eastern origins of his people. Mahan was convinced that the members of this tribe were both racially and linguistically different from other North American Indians. He believed that they had more in common with the Hebrews of ancient times, particularly in the area of religious mythology. There were striking parallels, Mahan asserted, between the Hebrew Feast of the Tabernacles and the Yuchi celebration of the harvest.

In 1966, Mahan learned that at least one other writer—diffusionist historian Charles Hapgood—shared his beliefs in outside influences on the Indian cultures of the region. He threw himself into a study of the Metcalf stone, hoping that the peculiar markings on the rock would provide the first hard evidence linking the Yuchi to the civilizations of the Old World. As luck would have it, proof of that connection—at least to his satisfaction—was already near at hand. When Manfred Metcalf had turned up in his office, Mahan was in the process of making a comparison between some pottery fragments unearthed in Georgia and the traditional designs used on Minoan ceramics. One of the reference works he was using in that study was a turn-of-the-century report on archaeological excavations in Crete, Sir Arthur Evans's *Palace of Minos.* And to Mahan's delight, nine of the symbols on the Metcalf stone were a perfect match with designs reproduced in Evans's book.

Mahan was reasonably satisfied that he was not dealing with a hoax. After all, he contended, the Metcalf stone had been a part of a house foundation that predated the publication of Sir Arthur Evans's book. Nevertheless, before going public with his findings, Mahan sought the opinions of other scholars who might verify his identification of the epigraphs. Predictably, several of his inquiries were summarily dismissed by the outside experts, who considered them utter nonsense. He was relieved to learn, therefore, that Cyrus Gordon was thoroughly intrigued by his theory. Gordon traveled to Georgia, studied the Metcalf stone, and confidently pronounced it genuine. When Mahan announced the discovery, he found out that Manfred Metcalf was not the only one who had stumbled on a curious inscribed rock in that region. During the months that followed, Mahan was contacted about more than twenty-five comparable finds, some of which he judged worthy of additional study.

One that was particularly intriguing was a small lead tablet unearthed in a flower bed some years earlier by Mrs. Joe Hearn of La Grange, Georgia. When one of Mrs. Hearn's relatives got in touch with Mahan, he was interested enough to excavate the site where the tablet had been found. In the process, he discovered evidence of small charcoal fires and lead spills, typical of a very old smelting works. To eliminate the possibility of any more contemporary explanation for the presence of the lead tablet, Mahan investigated the history of recent land use in the area. He found that prior to Mrs. Hearn's tenancy, the grounds had been farmland as far back as 1850; there was no indication that the land had been occupied before that time.

Mahan's research into the tablet itself convinced him that it was similar to those used by Babylonian merchants in the third century BC to record financial transactions. He believes that Mrs. Hearn's discovery is the oldest artifact ever found in the Americas.

Joseph Mahan is not as well known as Barry Fell, but he has attracted a significant following among diffusionist historians in the years since the Metcalf and Hearn artifacts came to light. In 1983, he was instrumental in founding the Institute for the Study of American Cultures. Mahan's organization takes a resolutely open-minded approach to the study of history, but it begins with the assumption that there remains "no reasonable doubt" that the peoples of Europe, Asia, and Africa traveled freely to and from the Americas.

At about the same time that Mahan was making public the Metcalf and Hearn inscriptions, Cyrus Gordon was stirring up the archaeological stewpot with another highly controversial pronouncement. According to Gordon, he had proof that the Phoenicians had been trading in South America a thousand years before the arrival of the conquistadors. The proof to which he was referring had to do with the so-called Paraíba stone, an artifact notorious for its rather checkered past.

The modern history of the Paraíba stone began in September 1872, when the viscount of Sapucaia, who was also president of the Instituto Historico y Geografico in Rio de Janeiro, received a brief letter from a man who identified himself as a plantation owner. The message read in part: "As I was having stones moved on my property of Pouso Alto, near the Paraíba [River], my slaves brought me one which they had already broken into four pieces. That stone bore numerous characters which no one understood. I had them copied by my son who knows a bit of draughtmanship, and I decided to send this copy to Your Excellency . . . to see whether Your Excellency or someone else can find out what these letters mean." The letter was signed, "Your Excellency's Attentive, devoted and obliged servant Joaquim Alves da Costa." Enclosed with the letter were renderings of the strange inscription.

The viscount's curiosity was piqued, and he called the matter to the attention of Dom Pedro II, emperor of Brazil, who was an ardent antiquary. Dom Pedro had no idea what the inscription might mean, but he was eager to find out and offered to underwrite the cost of additional study. The viscount therefore called upon Ladislau Netto, director of the Museo Nacional in Rio. Netto was a naturalist by profession and not a specialist in old stone epigraphs, but he was a gifted scholar who was generally knowledgeable about ancient history.

Unfortunately, no one could locate Alves da Costa or the Paraíba stone, and Netto was forced to pursue his research armed with only the hand-rendered copy of the inscription. For a period of months, he immersed himself in the study of Canaanite languages, before concluding that the mysterious characters were a form of Phoenician script. As best Netto could translate the text, it celebrated a voyage in the sixth century BC by intrepid Sidonian mariners. The sailors had embarked in ten ships from the Red Sea port of Ezion-geber, intent on sailing clear around Africa—the same mission attributed to explorers from Tarshish by the Greek chronicler Herodotus. According to Netto, the inscription described the travails of a ship that grew hopelessly lost and eventually made its way to the coast of Brazil with fifteen aboard still alive.

Netto hoped to rally scholarly corroboration for his views before publishing his findings on the Paraíba stone, but he also feared losing credit for his research if he revealed too much too soon. He decided, therefore, to send selected portions of his translation to Ernest Renan, a leading European authority on Canaanite epigraphy. Renan's reaction was a great disappointment, however, for he declared that the inscription was most likely a forgery. In support of this view, he cited certain features of the Canaanite text that did not fit the patterns for Canaanite grammar and word usage. Nevertheless, Netto was not persuaded. Disregarding Renan's criticism, he published a full report of his studies in 1873. Unfortunately, patron Dom Pedro had also been apprised of Renan's view and promptly withdrew his support. Netto's Brazilian colleagues followed suit, and in a matter of weeks the once-esteemed naturalist was reduced to a laughingstock.

In an effort to salvage his reputation, Netto tried once again to track down the elusive Joaquim Alves da Costa, but the little information that he had to guide him proved to be insufficient. Not only were there two Paraíba rivers in Brazil—one in the north and the other far away in the south—but there were several places called Pouso Alto. Netto eventually concluded that he had indeed been duped and admitted his error in too readily accepting the scanty evidence presented to him. The poor man lived out the remainder of his life under something of an academic cloud.

For nearly a century, Netto's tribulations were largely forgotten. But in 1967, a friend of Cyrus Gordon's, named Jules Piccus, acquired an old scrapbook at a neighborhood rummage sale. In the book, Piccus found a previously unknown letter from Netto, composed in 1874. The missive was addressed to Wilberforce Eames, a young American newspaperman; it was written in response to the reporter's queries regarding the Paraíba stone. Along with the letter, Netto had enclosed a tracing of the transcription on which he had based his ill-fated research.

Piccus forwarded a photostat of the newly discovered tracing to Gordon, who was struck by the differences between this version and the copies he had seen reproduced in nineteenth-century academic journals. Those versions,

The profile of a Phoenician oarsman (below), carved in Assyria in the seventh century BC, bears an uncanny resemblance to the image on a pre-Columbian incense burner (inset) found in Guatemala. The likeness has convinced some scholars that the burner's creator met a far-ranging Mediterranean mariner.

Gordon conceded, had not inspired confidence in Netto's Canaanite assignment. But the Eames version would seem to change everything. As Gordon explained, "The linguistic oddities that have cast suspicion on the text actually support its genuineness." What Renan and others had dismissed as evidence of forgery were idiosyncratic forms of expression, gender usages, and cryptographic tricks that would not be recognized as characteristic of certain Semitic dialects until well into this century. Unfortunately, such apparent corroboration came too late to brighten Netto's bitter final years. It also left the majority of mainstream historians no more convinced than before.

Right or wrong, Gordon's reaffirmation of Netto's Phoenician theory strikes a lively chord among some radical diffusionists. If the theory is correct, it would provide—among other things—a reasonable explanation for the legends that circulated among the Indians of Central and South America about a tall, bearded, white god who would one day return to redeem his followers.

The best known of these legends were the stories of Quetzalcoatl, the feathered serpent god of Mexico, and Viracocha, the god of the Incas, who was invariably described as having physical traits that were closer to those of a European than to those of the Indians. The god, Gordon believes, was nothing more than an explorer from the Middle East, whose knowledge and technical skills were so advanced relative to those of the Indians that they gave the visitor an air of divinity. When the Phoenician returned home, perhaps promising that he would visit again, it was only natural for the Indians to build up overblown expectations of the second coming.

Pre-Columbian transoceanic contacts with Central and South America would also help explain some of the curious anomalies observable in portrait sculptures and bas-relief architectural details from ancient ruins in those parts of the world. The faces depicted on some of these carvings are distinctly Negroid, Semitic, or European in their features, and the costumes portrayed in the artwork look distinctly foreign when compared to traditional Indian garb. Ancient visits from across the seas would also provide a reasonable explanation for the large collection of coral-encrusted amphorae that was dredged up from Guanabara Bay at Rio de Janeiro in 1982. The tall storage jars found in this unlikely location were of the same sort used to store provisions on Roman ships two centuries before the birth of Christ. An equally implausible find was an ancient Roman bust that was excavated from underneath several age-dated layers of earth near Mexico City.

The many nagging questions that remain about the early history of the Americas are a reminder that much of the story still awaits discovery. And as long as likely new clues—if genuine clues they are—keep turning up in pastures, flower beds, scrap heaps, and rummage sales, fresh diffusionist theories will probably continue to emerge. Until all the secrets are revealed, the struggle to decipher the past in the New World will doubtless remain a lively field of intellectual combat.

ACKNOWLEDGMENTS

The editors would like to thank the following for their assistance in the preparation of this volume: François Avril, Conservateur, Département des Manuscrits, Bibliothèque Nationale, Paris; William S. Ayres, Department of Anthropology, University of Oregon, Eugene; Professor Giorgio Bonamenti, Assisi, Italy; Warren Dexter, Rutland, Vermont; Professor Barry Fell, The Epigraphic Society, San Diego; Ida Jane Gallagher, Mount Pleasant, South Carolina; R. A. Gilbert, Bristol, England; Dr. George W. Gill, Professor of Anthropology, University of Wyoming, Laramie; David Lewis, University of Alaska, Anchorage; Toni Licari, Director, Runestone Museum, Alexandria, Minnesota; William R. McGlone, La Junta, Colorado; Christopher Rawlings, British Library, London; Wolfram Saida, Rathaus, Kernen, Germany; Erich von Däniken, Feldbrunnen, Switzerland.

BIBLIOGRAPHY

The Age of God-Kings (TimeFrame series). Alexandria, Va.: Time-Life Books, 1987.

Alcock, Leslie, *Was This Camelot? Excavations at Cadbury Castle 1966-1970.* New York: Stein and Day, 1972.

Ashe, Geoffrey, *Land to the West.* New York: Viking Press, 1962.

Ashe, Geoffrey, et al.:
The Quest for America. New York: Praeger, 1971.
The Quest for Arthur's Britain. New York: Frederick A. Praeger, 1968.

Ashton, Graham, *The Realm of King Arthur.* Newport, Isle of Wight, England: J. Arthur Dixon, 1974.

Ayres, William S., "Mystery Islets of Micronesia." *Archaeology,* January-February 1990.

Bacon, Edward, ed., *Vanished Civilizations of the Ancient World.* New York: McGraw-Hill, 1963.

Ballinger, Bill S., *Lost City of Stone.* New York: Simon and Schuster, 1978.

Barbarian Tides (TimeFrame series). Alexandria, Va.: Time-Life Books, 1987.

Begg, Paul:
"The Glastonbury Legend." *The Unexplained* (London), Vol. 9, Issue 99.
"The Lie of the Land." *The Unexplained* (London), Vol. 9, Issue 104.

Berlitz, Charles, *Mysteries from Forgotten Worlds.* Garden City, N.Y.: Doubleday, 1972.

Bond, Frederick Bligh, *The Gate of Remembrance.* New York: E. P. Dutton, 1933.

Bord, Janet, and Colin Bord, *The Secret Country.* London: Granada, 1979.

Bosi, Roberto, *The Lapps.* Transl. by James Cadell. New York: Frederick A. Praeger, 1960.

Breeden, Kay, and Stanley Breeden, "Eden in the Outback." *National Geographic,* February 1973.

Brookesmith, Peter, ed., *The Power of the Earth.* London: Orbis, 1984.

Caine, Mary, *Glastonbury Zodiac: Key to the Mysteries of Britain.* Torquay, Devon, England: Gravel Associates, 1978.

Campbell, Joseph:
Historical Atlas of World Mythology, Vol. 2. *The Way of the Seeded Earth,* Part 1: *The Sacrifice.* New York: Harper & Row, 1988.
The Mythic Image. Princeton, N.J.: Princeton University Press, 1981.
"A Canaanite Columbus?" *Newsweek,* October 26, 1970.

Canby, Thomas Y., "The Anasazi: Riddles in the Ruins." *National Geographic,* November 1982.

Canning, John, ed., *Great Unsolved Mysteries.* Secaucus, N.J.: Chartwell Books, 1984.

Capon, Edmund, *Art and Archaeology in China.* South Melbourne, Australia: Macmillan, 1977.

Carley, James P., *Glastonbury Abbey.* New York: St. Martin's Press, 1988.

Carlson, John B., "America's Ancient Skywatchers," *National Geographic,* March 1990.

Casson, Lionel, et al., *Mysteries of the Past.* Ed. by Joseph J. Thorndike, Jr. New York: American Heritage, 1977.

Catlin, George, *North American Indians: Being Letters and Notes on Their Manners, Customs, and Conditions, Written during Eight Years' Travel amongst the Wildest Tribes of Indians in North America, 1832-1839.* Vol. 2. Edinburgh: John Grant, 1926.

Cavendish, Richard, ed.:
Legends of the World. New York: Schocken Books, 1982.
Man, Myth & Magic. New York: Marshall Cavendish, 1985.
Mythology: An Illustrated Encyclopedia. London: Orbis, 1980.

Cazeau, Charles J., and Stuart D. Scott, Jr., *Exploring the Unknown.* New York: Plenum Press, 1979.

Cervé, Wishar S., and James D. Ward, *Lemuria: The Lost Continent of the Pacific.* San Jose, Calif.: Rosicrucian Press, 1931.

Charroux, Robert, *Forgotten Worlds.* Transl. by Lowell Bair. New York: Walker, 1973.

Childress, David Hatcher, *Lost Cities of Ancient Lemuria & the Pacific.* Stelle, Ill.: Adventures Unlimited Press, 1988.

Christian, F. W., *The Caroline Islands.* London: Methuen, 1899.

Christie, Anthony, *Chinese Mythology.* New York: Peter Bedrick Books, 1987.

Churchward, James, *The Lost Continent of Mu.* London: Neville Spearman, 1976.

Coe, Michael, *Mexico.* New York: Thames and Hudson, 1984.

Coe, Michael, Dean Snow, and Elizabeth Benson, *Atlas of Ancient America.* New York: Facts on File, 1986.

Cohen, Daniel, *Mysterious Places.* New York: Dodd, Mead, 1969.

Collins, Roger, *The Basques.* New York: Basil Blackwell, 1987.

Collyns, Robin, *Did Spacemen Colonize the Earth?* Chicago: Henry Regnery, 1976.

Colombel, Pierre, and Loomis Dean, "The Still-Mysterious Rock Paintings of Tassili Plateau Reveal a Rich Culture in What Has Become Saharan Wasteland." *Smithsonian,* July 1975.

Corliss, William R., comp., *Ancient Man: A Handbook of Puzzling Artifacts.* Glen Arm, Md.: Sourcebook Project, 1978.

Cornell, James, *Lost Lands and Forgotten People.* New York: Sterling, 1978.

Cotterell, Arthur, *The Macmillan Illustrated Encyclopedia of Myths & Legends.* New York: Macmillan, 1989.

Cyr, Donald L., ed., *Exploring Rock Art.* Santa Barbara, Calif.: Stonehenge Viewpoint, 1989.

Davidson, Daniel Sutherland, *Memoirs of the American Philosophical Society.* Vol. 5. *Aboriginal Australian and Tasmanian Rock Carvings and Paintings.* Philadelphia: American Philosophical Society, 1936.

Davies, Nigel, *Voyagers to the New World.* New York: William Morrow, 1979.

De Camp, L. Sprague, *Lost Continents: The Atlantis Theme in History, Science, and Literature.* New York: Dover, 1970.

Delaney, Frank, *The Celts.* London: British Broadcasting Corporation Publications, 1986.

Dexter, Warren W., *Ogam Consaine and Tifinag Alphabets: Ancient Uses.* Rutland, Vt.: Academy Books, 1984.

Discovery of Lost Worlds. New York: American Heritage, 1979.

Donnan, Christopher B., *Moche Art of Peru.* Los Angeles: Museum of Cultural History, University of California, 1978.

Donnelly, Ignatius, *Atlantis: The Antediluvian World.* Ed. by Egerton Sykes. New York: Gramercy, 1949.

Dos Passos, John, *Easter Island.* Garden City, N.Y.: Doubleday, 1971.

Eliade, Mircea, *Australian Religions.* Ithaca, N.Y.: Cornell University Press, 1973.

Empires Besieged (TimeFrame series). Alexandria, Va.: Time-Life Books, 1988.

Englert, Sebastian, *Island at the Center of the World.* Transl. and ed. by William Mulloy. New York: Charles Scribner's Sons, 1970.

Farrell, R. T., ed., *The Vikings.* London: Phillimore, 1982.

Feats and Wisdom of the Ancients (Library of Curious and Unusual Facts). Alexandria, Va.: Time-Life Books, 1990.

Fell, Barry:
America B.C. New York: Simon & Schuster, 1976.
Bronze Age America. Boston: Little, Brown, 1982.

Fingerhut, Eugene R., *Who Discovered America?* Claremont, Calif.: Regina Books, 1984.

Firestone, Clark B., *The Coasts of Illusion: A Study of Travel Tales.* New York: Harper & Brothers, 1924.

Franch, José Alcina, *Pre-Columbian Art.* Transl. by I. Mark Paris. New York: Harry N. Abrams, 1983.

Frazier, Kendrick, "The Anasazi Sun Dagger." *Science 80,* November-December 1989.

Freeman, Michael, and Roger Warner, *Angkor: The Hidden Glories.* Boston: Houghton Mifflin, 1990.

Gallop, Rodney, *A Book of the Basques.* Reno: University of Nevada Press, 1970.

Gmelch, George, and Sharon Gmelch, "Nomads in the Cities." *Natural History,* February 1988.

Goodman, Jeffrey, *Psychic Archaeology.* New York: Berkley, 1977.

Goodrich, Norma Lorre, *King Arthur.* New York: Franklin Watts, 1986.

Goran, Morris, *The Modern Myth: Ancient Astronauts and UFOs.* New York: A. S. Barnes, 1978.

Gordon, Cyrus H.:
Before Columbus. New York: Crown, 1971.
Riddles in History. New York: Crown, 1974.

Greene, Vaughn M., *The Six Thousand Year-Old Space Suit*. Bend, Ore.: Maverick Publications, 1982.

Greif, Martin, *The Holiday Book*. New York: Main Street Press, 1978.

Gypsies: Wanderers of the World. Washington, D.C.: National Geographic Society, 1970.

Hadingham, Evan, *Early Man and the Cosmos*. London: William Heinemann, 1983.

Haining, Peter, *Ancient Mysteries*. Richmond, Victoria, Australia: Sidgwick & Jackson, 1977.

Harpur, James, and Jennifer Westwood, *The Atlas of Legendary Places*. New York: Weidenfeld & Nicolson, 1989.

Heyerdahl, Thor:
Aku-Aku. Chicago: Rand McNally, 1958.
Easter Island: The Mystery Solved. New York: Random House, 1989.
The Horizon Book of Lost Worlds. New York: American Heritage, 1962.

Howard-Gordon, Frances, *Glastonbury: Maker of Myths*. Glastonbury, Somerset, England: Gothic Image, 1982.

Ingpen, Robert, and Philip Wilkinson, *Encyclopedia of Mysterious Places*. New York: Penguin, 1990.

Ingstad, Helge, "Vinland Ruins Prove Vikings Found the New World." *National Geographic*, November 1964.

Into the Unknown. Pleasantville, N.Y.: Reader's Digest Association, 1981.

The ISAC Report. Vol. 4, No. 4, November-December. Columbus, Ga.

James, Alan, *Lapps: Reindeer Herders of Lapland*. Vero Beach, Fla.: Rourke Publications, 1989.

Kolosimo, Peter, *Spaceships in Prehistory*. Transl. by Lovett F. Edwards. Secaucus, N.J.: University Books, 1975.

Koudelka, Josef (photography), and Willy Guy (text), *Gypsies*. New York: Aperture, 1975.

Kubler, George, *The Art and Architecture of Ancient America*. New York: Penguin Books, 1984.

Lacy, Norris J., ed., *The Arthurian Encyclopedia*. New York: Peter Bedrick Books, 1986.

La Fay, Howard, *The Vikings*. Washington, D.C.: National Geographic Society, 1972.

LaJoux, Jean-Dominique, *The Rock Paintings of Tassili*. Transl. by G. D. Liversage. Cleveland: World, 1963.

Landsburg, Alan, and Sally Landsburg, *In Search of Ancient Mysteries*. New York: Bantam, 1974.

Laxalt, Robert, and William Albert, "Land of the Ancient Basques." *National Geographic*, August 1968.

Lewis, David, *We, the Navigators*. Honolulu: University Press of Hawaii, 1972.

Lhote, Henri, *The Search for the Tassili Frescoes*. Transl. by Alan Houghton Brodrick. London: Hutchinson, 1959.

Long, Michael E., and Gary Smith, "Utah's Rock Art: Wilderness Louvre." *National Geographic*, January 1980.

McGlone, William R., and Phillip M. Leonard, *Ancient Celtic America*. Fresno, Calif.: Pioneer, 1986.

Mahan, Joseph, *The Secret*. Columbus, Ga.: Joseph Mahan, 1983.

Mallows, Wilfrid, *The Mystery of the Great Zimbabwe*. New York: W. W. Norton, 1984.

Michell, John:
The New View over Atlantis. San Francisco: Harper & Row, 1986.
The Traveler's Key to Sacred England. New York: Alfred A. Knopf, 1988.

Miller, Russell, and the Editors of Time-Life Books, *Continents in Collision* (Planet Earth series). Alexandria, Va.: Time-Life Books, 1983.

Morison, Samuel Eliot, *The European Discovery of America*. New York: Oxford University Press, 1971.

Morley, Sylvanus Griswold, *The Ancient Maya*. Stanford, Calif.: Stanford University Press, 1956.

Mysteries of the Ancient Americas. Pleasantville, N.Y.: Reader's Digest Association, 1986.

Mystic Places (Mysteries of the Unknown series). Alexandria, Va.: Time-Life Books, 1987.

Mythology: An Illustrated Encyclopedia. London: Orbis, 1980.

Nicholson, Irene, *Mexican and Central American Mythology*. New York: Peter Bedrick Books, 1987.

Noorbergen, Rene, *Secrets of the Lost Races*. Indianapolis: Bobbs-Merrill, 1977.

Norman, Bruce, *Footsteps: Nine Archaeological Journeys of Romance and Discovery*. Topsfield, Mass.: Salem House, 1988.

Peoples and Places of the Past. Washington, D.C.: National Geographic Society, 1983.

Peterson, Natasha, *Sacred Sites: A Traveler's Guide to North America's Most Powerful, Mystical Landmarks*. Chicago: Contemporary Books, 1988.

Putnam, James, *Egyptology*. New York: Crescent Books, 1990.

Quest for the Past. Pleasantville, N.Y.: Reader's Digest Association, 1986.

Ramsay, Raymond H., *No Longer on the Map*. New York: Viking Press, 1972.

Rawson, Jessica, *Ancient China: Art and Archaeology*. London: British Museum Publications, 1980.

Renfrew, Colin, *Before Civilization*. New York: Alfred A. Knopf, 1973.

Rhys, John, *Celtic Folklore: Welsh and Manx*. New York: Arno Press, 1980 (reprint of 1901 edition).

Roberts, David, "Mali's Dogon People." *National Geographic*, October 1990.

Sabloff, Jeremy A., *The Cities of Ancient Mexico: Reconstructing a Lost World*. New York: Thames and Hudson, 1989.

"Samurai Anthropologist." *Discover*, September 1989.

Schiffeler, John W., "Chinese Folk Medicine: A Study of the Shan-hai Ching." *Asian Folklore Studies*, 1980, Vol. 39, No. 2.

Scott-Elliot, W., *Legends of Atlantis and Lost Lemuria*. Wheaton, Ill.: Theosophical Publishing House, 1990.

Sitchin, Zecharia, *The 12th Planet*. New York: Stein and Day, 1976.

Slessarev, Vsevolod, *Prester John*. Minneapolis: University of Minnesota Press, 1959.

Smith, Gary, and Michael E. Long, "Utah's Art Galleries in Stone." *National Geographic*, January 1980.

Steiger, Brad, *Worlds Before Our Own*. New York: Berkley, 1978.

Stelle, Robert D., *The Sun Rises*. Ramona, Calif.: Lemurian Fellowship, 1952.

Stemman, Roy:
"Lemuria: A Likely Story?" *The Unexplained* (London), Vol. 10, Issue 115.
"Paradise Lost?" *The Unexplained* (London), Vol. 10, Issue 113.

Stiebing, William H., Jr., *Ancient Astronauts, Cosmic Collisions*. Buffalo: Prometheus Books, 1984.

Story, Ronald:
Guardians of the Universe? New York: St. Martin's Press, 1980.
The Space-Gods Revealed. New York: Harper & Row, 1976.

Strange Stories, Amazing Facts. Pleasantville, N.Y.: Reader's Digest Association, 1977.

Sullivan, Michael, *The Arts of China* (3rd ed.). Berkeley: University of California Press, 1984.

Thorndike, Joseph J., Jr., ed.:
Lost Worlds. New York: American Heritage, 1979.
Mysteries of the Past. New York: American Heritage, 1977.

Van Zandt, Eleanor, and Roy Stemman, *Mysteries of the Lost Lands*. London: Aldus Books, 1976.

von Däniken, Erich:
In Search of Ancient Gods. Transl. by Michael Heron. New York: G. P. Putnam's Sons, 1974.
Pathways to the Gods. Transl. by Michael Heron. New York: G. P. Putnam's Sons, 1982.

Wahlgren, Erik, *The Vikings and America*. London: Thames and Hudson, 1986.

Westwood, Jennifer, ed., *The Atlas of Mysterious Places*. New York: Weidenfeld & Nicholson, 1987.

White, Peter T., "Ancient Glory in Stone." *National Geographic*, May 1982.

PICTURE CREDITS

England. 46: From *The Atlas of Mysterious Places,* Jennifer Westwood, ed., Weidenfeld & Nicolson, New York, 1987—Mary Caine, Kingston, Surrey, England (2). 49: Courtesy the Trustees of the British Library, London. 50: Erich Lessing/Culture and Fine Arts Archive, Vienna; Philip Rahtz, York, England; courtesy the Trustees of the British Museum, London. 52, 53: Janet and Colin Bord, Clwyd, Wales. 54: Skyscan, Cheltenham, England; from *Glastonbury: Maker of Myths* by Frances Howard Gordon, Gothic Image Publications, Glastonbury, England, 1982. 55: Aerofilms, Boreham Wood, Herts, England. 57: Art Resource, New York. 58, 59: Trudy Pearson, Alexandria, Virginia. 60: Psychic News; from *The Gate of Remembrance* by Frederick Bligh Bond, E. P. Dutton, New York, 1918—Janet and Colin Bord, Clwyd, Wales. 62: Courtesy the Trustees of the British Library, London. 63: From *The Voiage and Travails of Sir John Maundevile, Kt.,* Edward Lumley, London, 1839 (reprinted from 1725 edition). 64, 65: Archiv der Gemeinde Kernan/Remstal; Robert Aberman/Barbara Heller, London—Walter M. Edwards, National Geographic Society. 66: Robert Aberman/Barbara Heller, London—courtesy the Trustees of the British Library, London. 69: Michael Freeman, London. 70, 71: Nihon Denpa News, Ltd., Tokyo; Michael Freeman, London (2). 72, 73: Thompson & Thompson, Tony Stone Worldwide, Chicago; Walter Rawlings/Robert Harding Picture Library, London—Robert Ingpen, Geelong, Victoria, Australia. 74, 75: Jane Taylor, Sonia Halliday Photographs, Buckinghamshire, England; ZEFA, Düsseldorf, Germany. 76, 77: © Wolfgang Kaehler

1990 (2)—Erich Lessing, Vienna. 78, 79: Paolo Koch, ZEFA, London; Forschungsprojekt Mohenjo-Daro, Aachen Foto Helmes—Robert Harding Picture Library, London. 80: David L. Brill, Fairburn, Georgia; from *The Anasazi* by J. J. Brody, Jaca Books, Milan, Italy, 1990, photo by Dudley W. King—courtesy Museum of Indian Arts and Culture/Laboratory of Anthropology, Santa Fe, New Mexico. 81: M. P. F. Fogden/Bruce Coleman Ltd., London. 83: Photri, Falls Church, Virginia. 84-89: George Holton/Photo Researchers, New York. 91: From *The Kon-Tiki Man* by Thor Heyerdahl, BBC Books, London, 1990. 92: Fotograf Ornelund, Oslo, Norway (3). 93: Gyldendal Norsk Forlag, Oslo, Norway—Bo-Aje Mellin, courtesy The Kon-Tiki Museum, Oslo, Norway (3). 94: Nadine Saunier/Rapho, Paris. 96: The Peabody Museum, Harvard University, Cambridge, Massachusetts, photo by Burger, 1991. 97: Courtesy the Trustees of the British Museum, London. 98: Hutchison Library, London. 99: Artwork by Fred Holtz—from *We, the Navigators: The Ancient Art of Landfilling in the Pacific* by David Lewis, University of Hawaii Press, Honolulu, 1975. 100, 101: David Herbig/Delimont, Herbig & Associates, Seattle; from *Lost City of Stone: The Story of Nan Madol, the "Atlantis" of the Pacific* by Bill S. Ballinger, Simon and Schuster, New York, 1978. 103: Fred Ward/Black Star. 104: Courtesy Department Library Services, American Museum of Natural History, New York—The University Museum, University of Pennsylvania, Philadelphia (neg. #T4-132c3). 105: Cultural Relics Publishing House, Beijing. 106: The Brooklyn Museum; from *Historical Atlas of World*

Mythology, Volume 2 by Joseph Campbell, Harper & Row, New York, 1988, photo by Michael Holford, London. 107: Otto E. Nelson, The Asia Society, New York, Mr. and Mrs. John D. Rockefeller 3rd Collection; Cultural Relics Publishing House, Beijing. 108: Warren W. Dexter, Rutland, Vermont—Kjell Sandved, Washington, D.C. 109: Shanghai Museum, Shanghai. 110: Loren McIntyre, Arlington, Virginia; from *Arte Precolombino de Ecuador,* Salvat Editores, Quito, Ecuador, 1985. 111: Cultural Relics Publishing House, Beijing—The Commercial Press, Hong Kong. 112: Jean Mazenod, "L'Art Précolombien," Éditions Citadelles, Paris. 113: To-Ji, Kyoto, Japan. 115: Walter T. Eitel, Randolph, New Hampshire. 116: J. Barnell/Superstock—Harald Sund, Seattle. 118, 119: All David L. Brill, Fairburn, Georgia, except sundial series, artwork by Fred Holtz. 121: Cotion Carlson, Brendan Archive, Brighton, Sussex—Brendan Archive, Brighton, Sussex. 122: The Arnamagnaeansk Institut, Copenhagen, Denmark. 125: From *North American Indian Portfolio* by George Catlin, 1844, Rare Book Division, Library of Congress, Washington, D.C. 127: From *Ancient Celtic America* by William R. McGlone and Phillip M. Leonard, Pioneer, Fresno, California, 1986—© David Muench 1991. 129: B. Anthony Stewart © National Geographic Society. 132: Warren W. Dexter, Rutland, Vermont—Ida Jane Gallagher, Mount Pleasant, South Carolina—from *Ancient Celtic America* by William R. McGlone and Phillip M. Leonard, Pioneer, Fresno, California, 1986. 133-135: Artwork by Time-Life Books. 137: Michael Holford, London—Musée de l'Homme, Paris.

INDEX

Time-Life Books is a division of Time Life Inc.,
a wholly owned subsidiary of
THE TIME INC. BOOK COMPANY

TIME-LIFE BOOKS

Managing Editor: Thomas H. Flaherty
Director of Editorial Resources: Elise D. Ritter-Clough
Director of Photography and Research: John Conrad Weiser
Editorial Board: Dale M. Brown, Roberta Conlan, Laura
Foreman, Lee Hassig, Jim Hicks, Blaine Marshall, Rita
Thievon Mullin, Henry Woodhead

PUBLISHER: Joseph J. Ward

Associate Publisher: Ann M. Mirabito
Editorial Director: Russell B. Adams, Jr.
Marketing Director: Anne Everhart
Director of Design: Louis Klein
Production Manager: Prudence G. Harris
Supervisor of Quality Control: James King

Editorial Operations
Production: Celia Beattie
Library: Louise D. Forstall
Computer Composition: Deborah G. Tait (Manager),
Monika D. Thayer, Janet Barnes Syring, Lillian Daniels

Library of Congress Cataloging in Publication Data
Mysterious Lands and Peoples / by the editors of Time-
Life Books.
    p. cm.—(Mysteries of the unknown)
Includes bibliographical references and index.
ISBN 0-8094-6520-5   ISBN 0-8094-6521-3 (library)
1. History—Miscellanea.
I. Time-Life Books.   II. Series.
D21.3.97 1991
902—dc20
                                        91-10278
                                        CIP

MYSTERIES OF THE UNKNOWN

SERIES EDITOR: Jim Hicks
Series Administrator: Jane A. Martin
Art Director: Ellen Robling
Picture Editor: Susan V. Kelly

Editorial Staff for *Mysterious Lands and Peoples*
Text Editors: Robert A. Doyle (principal), Janet Cave
Senior Writer: Esther R. Ferington
Associate Editor/Research: Gwen C. Mullen
Assistant Editors/Research: Constance Contreras, Denise
Dersin
Assistant Art Director: Susan M. Gibas
Writers: Marfé Ferguson Delano, Sarah D. Ince
Senior Copy Coordinator: Colette Stockum
Copy Coordinator: Donna Carey
Picture Coordinator: Michael Kentoff
Editorial Assistant: Donna Fountain

Special Contributors: Susan M. Schaeffer (lead research);
Patricia A. Paterno, Evelyn S. Prettyman, Nancy J. Seeger,
Priscilla Tucker (research); John Clausen, George Consta-
ble, Kenneth C. Danforth, Alison Kahn, Gina Maranto,
Margery A. duMond, Wendy Murphy, Susan Perry (text);
Sara Schneidman (consultant); John Drummond (design);
Hazel Blumberg-McKee (index).

Correspondents: Elisabeth Kraemer-Singh (Bonn), Christine
Hinze (London), Christina Lieberman (New York), Maria
Vincenza Aloisi (Paris), Ann Natanson (Rome).
Valuable assistance was also provided by Li Yan (Beijing);
Barry Iverson (Cairo); Maria Helena Jervis (Ecuador); Bing
Wong (Hong Kong); Judy Aspinall (London); John Dunn
(Melbourne); Elizabeth Brown, Katheryn White (New
York); Dag Christensen (Oslo); Ann Wise (Rome); Dick
Berry, Mieko Ikeda (Tokyo).

Other Publications:
THE NEW FACE OF WAR
HOW THINGS WORK
WINGS OF WAR
CREATIVE EVERYDAY COOKING
COLLECTOR'S LIBRARY OF THE UNKNOWN
CLASSICS OF WORLD WAR II
TIME-LIFE LIBRARY OF CURIOUS AND UNUSUAL FACTS
AMERICAN COUNTRY
THE THIRD REICH
VOYAGE THROUGH THE UNIVERSE
THE TIME-LIFE GARDENER'S GUIDE
TIME FRAME
FIX IT YOURSELF
FITNESS, HEALTH & NUTRITION
SUCCESSFUL PARENTING
HEALTHY HOME COOKING
UNDERSTANDING COMPUTERS
LIBRARY OF NATIONS
THE ENCHANTED WORLD
THE KODAK LIBRARY OF CREATIVE PHOTOGRAPHY
GREAT MEALS IN MINUTES
THE CIVIL WAR
PLANET EARTH
COLLECTOR'S LIBRARY OF THE CIVIL WAR
THE EPIC OF FLIGHT
THE GOOD COOK
WORLD WAR II
HOME REPAIR AND IMPROVEMENT
THE OLD WEST

*For information on and a full description of any of the Time-
Life Books series listed above, please call 1-800-621-7026 or
write:*
Reader Information
Time-Life Customer Service
P.O. Box C-32068
Richmond, Virginia 23261-2068

This volume is one of a series that examines the history
and nature of seemingly paranormal phenomena. Other
books in the series include:

Mystic Places	*Powers of Healing*
Psychic Powers	*Search for the Soul*
The UFO Phenomenon	*Transformations*
Psychic Voyages	*Dreams and Dreaming*
Phantom Encounters	*Witches and Witchcraft*
Visions and Prophecies	*Time and Space*
Mysterious Creatures	*Magical Arts*
Mind over Matter	*Utopian Visions*
Cosmic Connections	*Secrets of the Alchemists*
Spirit Summonings	*Eastern Mysteries*
Ancient Wisdom and Secret Sects	*Earth Energies*
Hauntings	*Cosmic Duality*